History

FOR COMMON ENTRANCE

13+

Revision Guide

History

FOR COMMON ENTRANCE

13+

Revision Guide

Ed Adams

About the author

Ed Adams was educated at Sutton Valence School and the University of Exeter, where he gained degrees in Law and Medieval Studies. He lives in Kent.

Acknowledgements

I would like to thank all the staff at Galore Park for helping to make this possible, and most especially Frances and Emily.

Ed Adams

The publishers would like to thank the following for permission to reproduce copyright material:
Photo credits p.137 Mary Evans Picture Library/Alamy
Acknowledgements
Every effort has been made to trace all copyright holders, but if any have been inadvertently overlooked the publishers will be pleased to make the necessary arrangements at the first opportunity.

Although every effort has been made to ensure that website addresses are correct at time of going to press, Galore Park cannot be held responsible for the content of any website mentioned in this book. It is sometimes possible to find a relocated web page by typing in the address of the home page for a website in the URL window of your browser.

Hachette UK's policy is to use papers that are natural, renewable and recyclable products and made from wood grown in well-managed forests and other controlled sources.
The logging and manufacturing processes are expected to conform to the environmental regulations of the country of origin.

Orders: **Teachers** please contact Bookpoint Ltd, 130 Park Drive, Milton Park, Abingdon, Oxon OX14 4SE. Telephone: (44) 01235 400555. Email primary@bookpoint.co.uk. Lines are open from 9 a.m. to 5 p.m., Monday to Saturday, with a 24-hour message answering service

Parents, Tutors please call: 020 3122 6405 (Monday to Friday, 9:30 a.m. to 4.30 p.m.).Email: parentenquiries@galorepark.co.uk

Visit our website at www.galorepark.co.uk for details of other revision guides for Common Entrance, examination papers and Galore Park publications.

ISBN: 978 1 471809 02 6

First published by Galore Park Publishing Ltd
An Hachette UK company
Carmelite House
50 Victoria Embankment
London EC4Y 0DZ
www.galorepark.co.uk

First edition published 2009
Second edition published 2012
This edition:
Impression number 10 9
2020 2019

Typeset in 11.5/13 pt ITC Officina Sans by DC Graphic Design Limited, Swanley Village.
Illustrations by DC Graphic Design Limited, Swanley Village.
Cartoons by Ian Douglass
Printed in India

A catalogue record for this title is available from the British Library

Contents

Introduction x

Part A Medieval Realms: Britain 1066–1485 1

Chapter 1 **The Norman Conquest** 2
1.1 Background to the Conquest 2
1.2 Preparations for the invasion 2
1.3 The Battle of Stamford Bridge, 25 September 1066 4
1.4 The Battle of Hastings, 14 October 1066 5

Chapter 2 **Conquered England** 8
2.1 Medieval rule and the Feudal System 8
2.2 Revolts and rebellions 9
2.3 New buildings 9
2.4 The Domesday Book 10
2.5 Life in the manor 11

Chapter 3 **The sons of William I** 13
3.1 William II (1087–1100) 13
3.2 Henry I (1100–35) 13
3.3 Matilda 13
3.4 The Church 14
3.5 Monasteries and nunneries 15

Chapter 4 **From civil war to Henry II** 17
4.1 Stephen (1135–54) 17
4.2 Henry II (1154–89) 17
4.3 Thomas Becket 17
4.4 Eleanor of Aquitaine and the sons of Henry II 18

Chapter 5 **Richard I, the Crusades and King John** 20
5.1 The First Crusade 20
5.2 Richard I (1189–99) and the Third Crusade 21
5.3 John and the Angevin Empire 22
5.4 John and the Church 23
5.5 Magna Carta 23

Chapter 6 **Henry III and the Edwards** 25
6.1 Henry III (1216–72) 25
6.2 Edward I (1272–1307) 26
6.3 Wales and Scotland 26
6.4 Edward II (1307–27) 28
6.5 The fall of Edward II 28
6.6 Edward III (1327–77) 29
6.7 The Battle of Crécy, 26 August 1346 30
6.8 The last years of Edward III 31

Chapter 7 Life in the Middle Ages 33
7.1 Castles 33
7.2 The Jews 35
7.3 Medieval women 36
7.4 Medieval health and the Black Death 36

Chapter 8 Richard II and life in the towns 38
8.1 Richard II (1377–99) and the Peasants' Revolt 38
8.2 The fall of Richard II 39
8.3 Towns 39
8.4 Guilds 40
8.5 Town government, law and order 40

Chapter 9 The three Henrys 42
9.1 Henry IV (1399–1413) 42
9.2 Henry V (1413–22) 42
9.3 The Battle of Agincourt, 25 October 1415 43
9.4 Joan of Arc 44
9.5 Henry VI (1422–71) 45
9.6 The coming of civil war 46

Chapter 10 The Wars of the Roses 48
10.1 The first war (1459–61) 48
10.2 Edward IV (1461–83) 49
10.3 The second war (1470–71) 50
10.4 Edward V and Richard III (1483–85) 51
10.5 The Battle of Bosworth, 22 August 1485 52

Part B The Making of the United Kingdom: 1485–1750 55

Chapter 11 Henry VII (1485–1509) 56
11.1 Securing the throne 56
11.2 The two pretenders 57
11.3 The tax rebellions 58
11.4 Foreign policy 58

Chapter 12 Henry VIII (1509–47) 60
12.1 Early life and reign 60
12.2 Thomas Wolsey 60
12.3 The rise of Protestantism 61
12.4 The King's Great Matter 62
12.5 Cromwell and the Reformation 63
12.6 The six wives of Henry VIII 65

Chapter 13 Edward VI (1547–53) and Mary I (1553–58) 68
13.1 Edward VI and the Protestant surge 68
13.2 Lady Jane Grey and Mary I 69
13.3 Wyatt's Rebellion (1554) 70
13.4 The Catholic resurgence 70

Chapter 14	**Elizabeth I (1558–1603)**	**72**
	14.1 Early life and reign	72
	14.2 The Elizabethan Settlement	73
	14.3 Mary, Queen of Scots	74
	14.4 War with Spain	75
	14.5 Elizabeth's government	77
Chapter 15	**Life in the sixteenth century**	**80**
	15.1 Trade	80
	15.2 Poverty and the Poor Laws	80
	15.3 Town and country	82
	15.4 Women in the sixteenth century	83
Chapter 16	**James I (1603–25) and Charles I (1625–49)**	**85**
	16.1 James I and religion	85
	16.2 James I and Parliament	86
	16.3 Charles I and religion	87
	16.4 Charles I and Parliament	87
	16.5 Causes of the Civil War	88
Chapter 17	**Civil War (1642–49) and the Interregnum (1649–60)**	**91**
	17.1 The English Civil War	91
	17.2 The Battle of Marston Moor, 2 July 1644	92
	17.3 Oliver Cromwell and the New Model Army	93
	17.4 The trial and execution of Charles I	94
	17.5 Cromwell and Parliament	94
	17.6 Ireland and Scotland	95
	17.7 Richard Cromwell and the Restoration	96
Chapter 18	**Charles II (1660–85) and James II (1685–88)**	**98**
	18.1 Charles II	98
	18.2 Plague and fire	98
	18.3 Charles II and religion	100
	18.4 James II and the Monmouth Rebellion	101
	18.5 The Glorious Revolution	101
	18.6 Culture and science	102
Chapter 19	**William III and Mary II (1689–1702) and Anne (1702–14)**	**105**
	19.1 William III and Mary II	105
	19.2 Ireland and France	105
	19.3 The Act of Settlement (1701)	106
	19.4 Anne and war with France	106
	19.5 The Battle of Blenheim, 13 August 1704	106
	19.6 The Act of Union (1707)	107
Chapter 20	**George I (1714–27) and George II (1727–60)**	**109**
	20.1 George I and the 1715 Jacobite Rebellion	109
	20.2 Parliament and Walpole	109
	20.3 Trade and the empire	110
	20.4 George II and war with Europe	111
	20.5 The 1745 Jacobite Rebellion	111

Part C Britain and Empire: 1750–1914 115

Chapter 21 The Seven Years' War 116
21.1 Background 116
21.2 William Pitt the Elder 116
21.3 Wolfe and the fall of Quebec 117
21.4 British victories and the end of the campaign 118

Chapter 22 The American Rebellion and World War 120
22.1 Background 120
22.2 The outbreak of war 121
22.3 The early war 123
22.4 The later war 124

Chapter 23 The French Revolution and the Napoleonic Wars 126
23.1 The French Revolution 126
23.2 William Pitt the Younger 126
23.3 Horatio Nelson 127
23.4 The Trafalgar campaign 128
23.5 Arthur Wellesley, Duke of Wellington 129
23.6 The Waterloo campaign 129

Chapter 24 Dissent and calls for political reform, 1815–48 132
24.1 The rise of protest 132
24.2 The Reform Acts 133
24.3 Chartism 134

Chapter 25 The Agricultural and Industrial Revolutions 136
25.1 The Agricultural Revolution 136
25.2 The Industrial Revolution 137
25.3 Public health 139

Chapter 26 The transportation revolution 141
26.1 Roads 141
26.2 Canals 141
26.3 Rail 142
26.4 Telford and Brunel 143

Chapter 27 Social and industrial reform 145
27.1 The slave trade 145
27.2 The abolition movement 145
27.3 Prison reform 147
27.4 Poor Law reform 147
27.5 Employment reform 147

Chapter 28 Religious life, 1750–1914 150
28.1 Catholicism and the Oxford Movement 150
28.2 Methodism and the Evangelical movement 152

Chapter 29 Victorian England: success, war and politics 154
29.1 Victoria's life 154
29.2 Victorian politics 154
29.3 The Great Exhibition 156

29.4 The Crimean War 156
29.5 Seacole and Nightingale 157
29.6 Women's suffrage 158

Chapter 30 The British Empire and the road to war 161
30.1 India 161
30.2 The Indian Mutiny 162
30.3 South Africa 164
30.4 The Anglo-Boer War, 1899–1902 164
30.5 Great Power rivalries, 1871–1914 167

Essay question answers 169

Test yourself answers 177

Appendix 1 – Timelines 184
The monarchs of England, 1066–1485 184
The monarchs of England, 1485–1750 185
The monarchs of Great Britain and the United Kingdom, 1750–1900 186

Appendix 2 – Family trees 187
For Chapters 1–2 187
For Chapters 3–5 188
For Chapter 6 189
For Chapters 8–11 190
For Chapters 12–14 191
For Chapters 16–20 192
For Chapters 21–30 193

Introduction

This revision guide covers all three periods of the ISEB History syllabus for Common Entrance at 13+.

The material is arranged according to the structure set out in *History for Common Entrance: Medieval Realms Britain 1066–1485*, *History for Common Entrance: The Making of the UK 1485–1750*, and *History for Common Entrance: Britain and Empire 1750–1914*, following a strictly chronological format. This, we believe, is the clearest, simplest and most useful way of learning the subject, and we hope it works for you.

This book will give you all the facts you need to know, and you should learn them thoroughly, but your success in the exam will depend on what you do with these facts. Do read the section below, which will give you advice on how to write strong answers in the exam and how to revise most effectively.

You will also find many opportunities throughout this book to test both your knowledge of the facts and your skill at writing answers.

History is a fascinating subject but has gained a reputation for being one of the harder ones to tackle. It can certainly be challenging, but need not be impossible. A good grasp of the skills that make a good historian will show your future teachers – and perhaps, future employers – that you have the necessary discipline to succeed in plenty of areas.

So make the most of this opportunity to show them. Good luck!

How to use this book

- Throughout this book you will find revision tips. These will give you suggestions about different tools you can use to help you remember the key facts/events/dates, and so on. Everybody learns differently and these boxes will give you some ideas on different approaches you can use. Although they are only suggestions, they will hopefully help you think of different ways that work for you. All these tips are taken from *Study Skills* by Elizabeth Holtom, published by Galore Park, and you can get details of all the different suggestions, as well as finding out what sort of learner you are, from that book.
- Read a page of this book, then cover it up and write down as many of the ideas as you can remember. Then look at the page again.
- Once you have finished reading a chapter, try the 'Test yourself' questions. This will show whether you have remembered the historical facts. Check your answers against those at the back of the book. Keep doing this over time to check that you have retained the information.
- Try the sample essay questions. These are written in exactly the same way as the questions in the exam. Suggested answers are given at the back of the book.
- Use the family trees (see pages 187–193) to see how the important historical figures are related to each other. This will help you to understand the tricky issues surrounding royal succession.
- Practice makes perfect, so get a copy of *History for Common Entrance 13+ Exam Practice Questions*. It contains over a hundred evidence and essay questions, giving you plenty of opportunity to develop your answer-writing skills.

The syllabus and your exams

For Common Entrance History, you will sit an exam lasting an hour, for which you will need to answer one question from Section 1 and one question from Section 2.

Section 1: the evidence question

- The evidence question is worth 20 marks and it is recommended that you spend five minutes reading the sources and 20 minutes writing your answer to the question.
- You will be presented with three sources. These may include an entry from a historical chronicle, an extract from a book written by a modern historian or a piece of correspondence from the time. At least one of the sources will be pictorial, either produced at the time or a modern reconstruction.
- The question will ask you to look at all the sources *and use your own knowledge* in order to answer it. So it will help you to give a strong, full answer if you know at least a little about the topic, for example the background to it, the events of the time and any future consequences.
- In answering the question you will need to consider the reliability of each source. To do this effectively you will need to understand the issues of **provenance**, **first-hand evidence** and **hindsight**.
- **Provenance** is the issue of where a source comes from. An account of the Battle of Hastings written by a Norman source would be very different from one written by an English source. A Norman author would write from a winner's perspective. He might exaggerate the bravery and skill of the Norman soldiers, or the cowardice and incompetence of the English. An English writer would write from a loser's perspective, and might argue that the Normans won purely by luck and that the battle was a great tragedy for England.
- **First-hand evidence** is that produced by an author who was actually present at the events described. An author who actually fought at the Battle of Hastings might write differently from an author who heard about the battle from another person. Sometimes authors write based on folk tales that have been passed through hundreds of people. Detail can be lost and exaggerations added. But a story that has been passed on before being written down may still have important things to say about another person's perception of events.
- **Hindsight** is the knowledge gained about an event after it has taken place. An author writing on the day after the Battle of Hastings might write differently from an author writing a hundred or even a thousand years later, who does so with the benefit of hindsight. Sometimes details may be forgotten or changed over time. But don't assume that a source will always be less reliable because a lot of time has passed. Modern historians – who generally write a long time after the event – can have a better overall view of the historical events.
- When you consider each source, you will need to look at these issues and see which ones are relevant. It is important to remember that there is often no 'right' or 'wrong' answer. You are being asked to argue your opinion, based on the evidence presented.

Section 2: the essay question

- The essay question is worth 30 marks and it is recommended that you spend 35 minutes on it.
- You will have a wide variety of questions to choose from and they may be applied to any topic of your choice.
- The questions are worded in a few ways but generally you will be asked to 'explain'.
- When you are asked to 'explain' you will still need to know the historical facts and understand the chronology of the events.
- It will help to include the dates of the events you describe. This will prove to the examiner that you have learnt the material properly and will earn you more marks.
- You should write your answer in the past tense.
- When you are asked to explain the reasons for something, you will need to consider why something happened and state your opinion, using sources to back up your claims.
- You need to look at the causes behind the event or the consequences of it.
- You will earn most marks for giving a balanced opinion. Try to argue two different opinions, then come to a conclusion where you reject one in favour of the other.
- There is never a 'right' or 'wrong' answer, only 'strong' and 'weak' ones. Another pupil could arrive at a completely different conclusion and receive the same number of marks. The examiner is looking for evidence that you understand the causes or consequences of an event, know how to analyse them properly and can back up your analysis by reference to the sources.
- When using historical sources to back up your claims, make sure you consider how reliable they are by considering provenance, first-hand evidence and hindsight. This could affect your conclusion.

Tips on revising

Get the best out of your brain

- Give your brain plenty of oxygen by exercising. You can revise effectively if you feel fit and well.
- Eat healthy food while you are revising. Your brain works better when you give it good fuel.
- Think positively. Give your brain positive messages so that it will want to study.
- Keep calm. If your brain is stressed it will not operate effectively.
- Take regular breaks during your study time.
- Get enough sleep. Your brain will carry on sorting out what you have revised while you sleep.

Get the most from your revision

- Don't work for hours without a break. Revise for 20–30 minutes then take a five-minute break.

- Do good things in your breaks: listen to your favourite music, eat healthy food, drink some water, do some exercise and juggle. Don't read a book, watch TV or play on the computer; it will conflict with what your brain is trying to learn.
- When you go back to your revision, review what you have just learnt.
- Regularly review the facts you have learnt.

Get motivated

- Set yourself some goals and promise yourself a treat when the exams are over.
- Make the most of all the expertise and talent available to you at school and at home. If you don't understand something ask your teacher to explain.
- Find a quiet place to revise and make sure you have all the equipment you need.
- Organise your time so that you revise all subjects equally.

Know what to expect in the exam

- Use past papers to familiarise yourself with the format of the exam.
- Make sure you understand the language examiners use.

Before the exam

- Have all your equipment and pens ready the night before.
- Make sure you are at your best by getting a good night's sleep before the exam.
- Have a good breakfast in the morning.
- Take some water into the exam if you are allowed.
- Think positively and keep calm.

During the exam

- Have a watch on your desk. Work out how much time you need to allocate to each question and try to stick to it.
- Make sure you read and understand the instructions and rules on the front of the exam paper.
- Allow some time at the start to read and consider the questions carefully before writing anything.
- Read all the questions at least twice. Don't rush into answering before you have a chance to think about it.
- If a question is particularly hard move on to the next one. Go back to it if you have time at the end.
- Check your answers make sense if you have time at the end.

For more tips on how to get the best from your revision and your exams, see *Study Skills* (9781902984599) by Elizabeth Holtom, published by Galore Park.

PART A
MEDIEVAL REALMS
BRITAIN 1066–1485

1 The Norman Conquest

1.1 Background to the Conquest

On the death of Edward the Confessor on 5 January 1066, three men claimed the crown of England:

- Harold Godwinson
- William, Duke of Normandy
- Harald Hardrada, King of Norway

Harold Godwinson

- The largest landholder in England and Edward's most powerful noble.
- Harold claimed that Edward had named him as his successor on his deathbed.
- The *Anglo-Saxon Chronicle* supports Harold's claim: 'The prudent King [Edward] had settled the kingdom on high-born men, on Harold himself, the noble Earl.'

William, Duke of Normandy

- The illegitimate son of Robert, Duke of Normandy, and distant cousin of Edward.
- William claimed that Edward had promised him the throne on a visit to England in 1052.
- William also claimed that Harold had sworn an oath over holy relics that he would support William's right to the English throne.

Harald Hardrada, King of Norway

- Harald was the King of Norway. He was supported by Harold's brother Tostig.
- Tostig argued that the English throne should have passed to King Magnus of Norway and then Hardrada after him.

Harold Godwinson was chosen as King by the Witan (the council of important earls and bishops) and crowned on 6 January 1066.

1.2 Preparations for the invasion

Harold spent the spring and summer of 1066 preparing for an invasion by William or Harald Hardrada.

- Harold remained in the south with his army, guarding the coast closest to France.
- Earls Edwin of Mercia and Morcar of Northumbria were left in the north with their army, to guard against a Viking invasion.

- By late summer, when there had been no sign of an invasion, the soldiers were keen to return home to gather their harvests.

William was also preparing for the invasion of England.

- First he had to convince his barons that the invasion was a good idea. Many wished to stay at home to look after their own lands.
- They were convinced by the promise of more lands in England and because William had managed to persuade Pope Alexander II to give his support.
- When William's fleet was gathered at Dives in late summer, the wind was blowing in the wrong direction. During September, William's army could only sit and wait for the wind to change.

Meanwhile, the wind was favourable for Harald Hardrada's army to sail from Norway.

- Hardrada's army defeated Edwin and Morcar at the Battle of Fulford on 20 September.
- He then went on to capture York and started pillaging the area.
- On hearing of the invasion, Harold decided to march his army north. They arrived to catch Hardrada by surprise, at Stamford Bridge near York.

Revision tip

Try mapping out the events running up to the Battle of Stamford Bridge to help you remember them. Start with Harold being crowned King, then have three branches, one for each of Harold, William and Harald. You might start it like the chart below. You will need to add some more sub-branches to cover all the key points. Try and use pictures instead of words where you can.

For help with producing a chart like this, see *Study Skills*, pages 43–48.

Events leading to Battle of Stamford Bridge

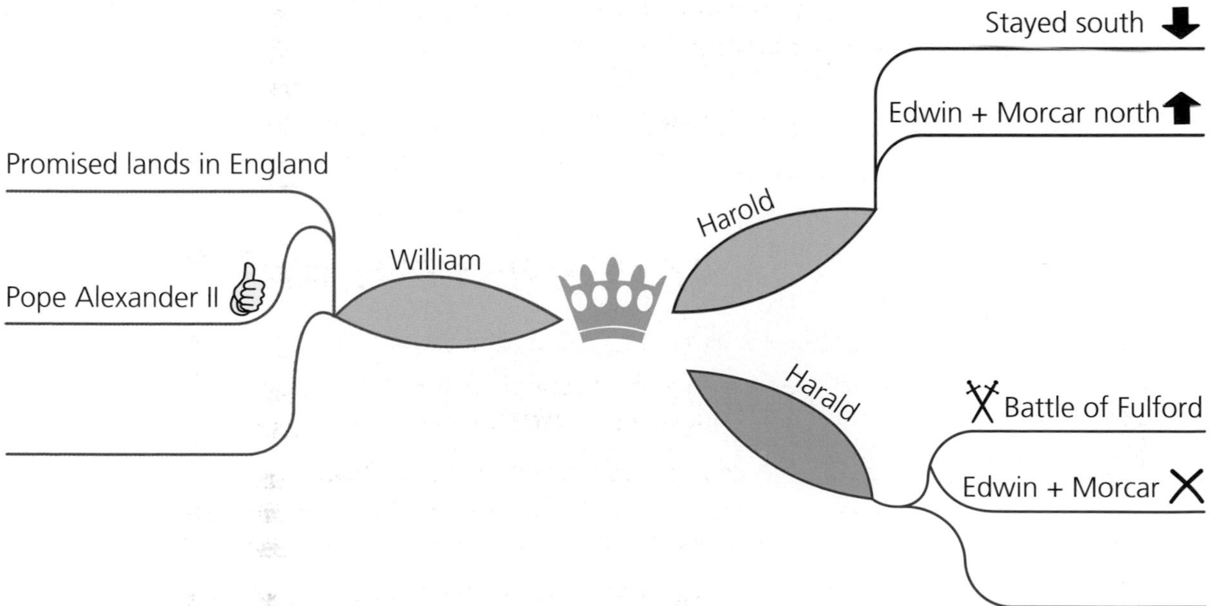

1.3 The Battle of Stamford Bridge, 25 September 1066

- As the English army approached, Hardrada led his army across a river to high ground. A small band of men was left to hold the bridge and delay the English for as long as possible.
- Hardrada formed his army into a shieldwall on the high ground.
- The archers and slingers in each army began by hurling missiles at each other.
- The English charged at the Vikings and were able to break up Hardrada's shieldwall.
- In the fighting, both Harald Hardrada and Tostig were killed.

Meanwhile, the wind had changed, allowing William's army to sail across the Channel.

- The Normans landed at Pevensey on 28 September. William's men were sent through the countryside, looting, burning and gathering food from the locals.
- Harold was still in the north when he found out about the Norman landing. His army was exhausted and many had been killed at Stamford Bridge.
- His brothers Leofwine and Gyrth advised him to rest and take time to build up a stronger force to fight the Normans. Harold, however, decided to march his army south straight away.
- Harold reached London on 6 October and continued south, while the Normans marched north from Pevensey to meet them.

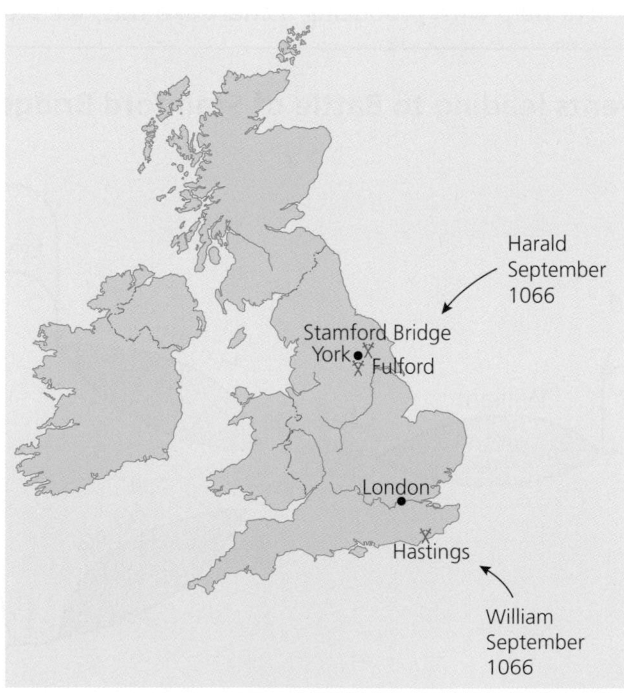

1.4 The Battle of Hastings, 14 October 1066

The two armies met on the morning of 14 October, at a place outside Hastings called Senlac Hill.

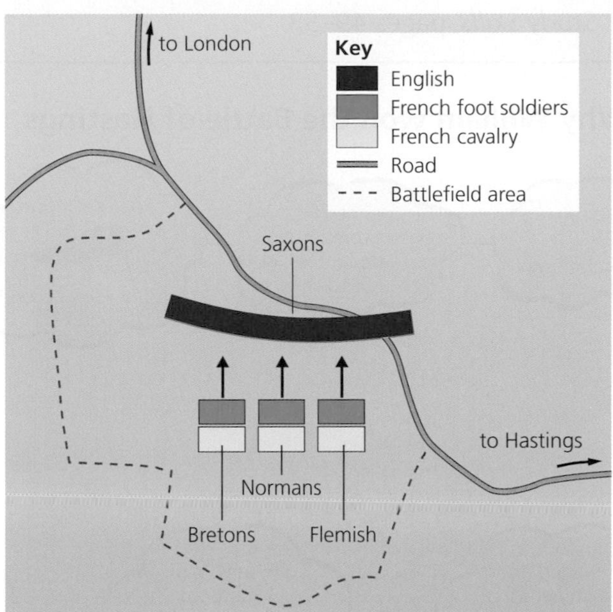

- The English formed a shieldwall along a ridge at the top of the hill.
- William's army formed three divisions in the valley below. The Bretons were on the left flank, Normans in the centre and Flemish on the right.
- The Norman archers began by firing into the English line. This had little effect as the English were well protected by their shields.
- Norman foot soldiers advanced up the hill to attack the English by hand, but they were unable to break the shieldwall.
- As the foot soldiers withdrew, the Norman knights advanced. Still the shieldwall held and the knights retreated.
- The Breton soldiers on the left flank of William's army decided to retreat hurriedly and ran back down the hill.
- When some of the ill-disciplined English fyrd broke ranks to follow the Bretons down the hill, the knights regrouped and killed them.
- As the English shieldwall was weakened, Harold's brothers Leofwine and Gyrth were killed.
- In one final assault in the late afternoon, the Normans managed to collapse the shieldwall and reach the King's position. In the midst of the fighting, Harold was killed.
- At Harold's death, the remaining English army fled. William marched to London, gaining support on his way, and was crowned King on Christmas Day, 1066.

Revision tip

Below is a flow chart showing why William won the Battle of Hastings rather than Harold. It summarises the key points, using abbreviated words and bubbles. To see how to produce a flow chart like this see *Study Skills*, pages 49–53.

Why William won the Battle of Hastings

WILLIAM
- determined + ambitious
- claimed H. had promised to help him → king
- Pope's support (Papal banner) army: God on our side
- thorough preps. for invasion thro' spring + summer 1066

WILLIAM'S LUCK
- waited all summer for winds → fleet → Eng. winds changed late Sept
- H. in N. ⚔ of Stamford Bridge v. King of Norway, Harald + Tostig
- W. + army ↓ Pevensey 28th Sept ↓ undefended coast

HAROLD'S ARMY
- exhausted ↓ fought + won ⚔ Stamford Bridge ↓ marched S. very quickly 180 miles in 4 days
- housecarls ↓ dead/wounded
- archers ↓ left behind
- Fyrd ↓ on foot ↓ untrained farmers ↓ brave but not well disciplined ↓ shieldwall

WILLIAM'S ARMY
- strong + disciplined ↓ ↓ ↓ archers infantry cavalry
- fake retreats ↓ tricked Fyrd ↓ shieldwall broken ↓ H. killed + Saxons fled
- **W. won after whole day fighting ↓ crowned Xmas Day 1066**

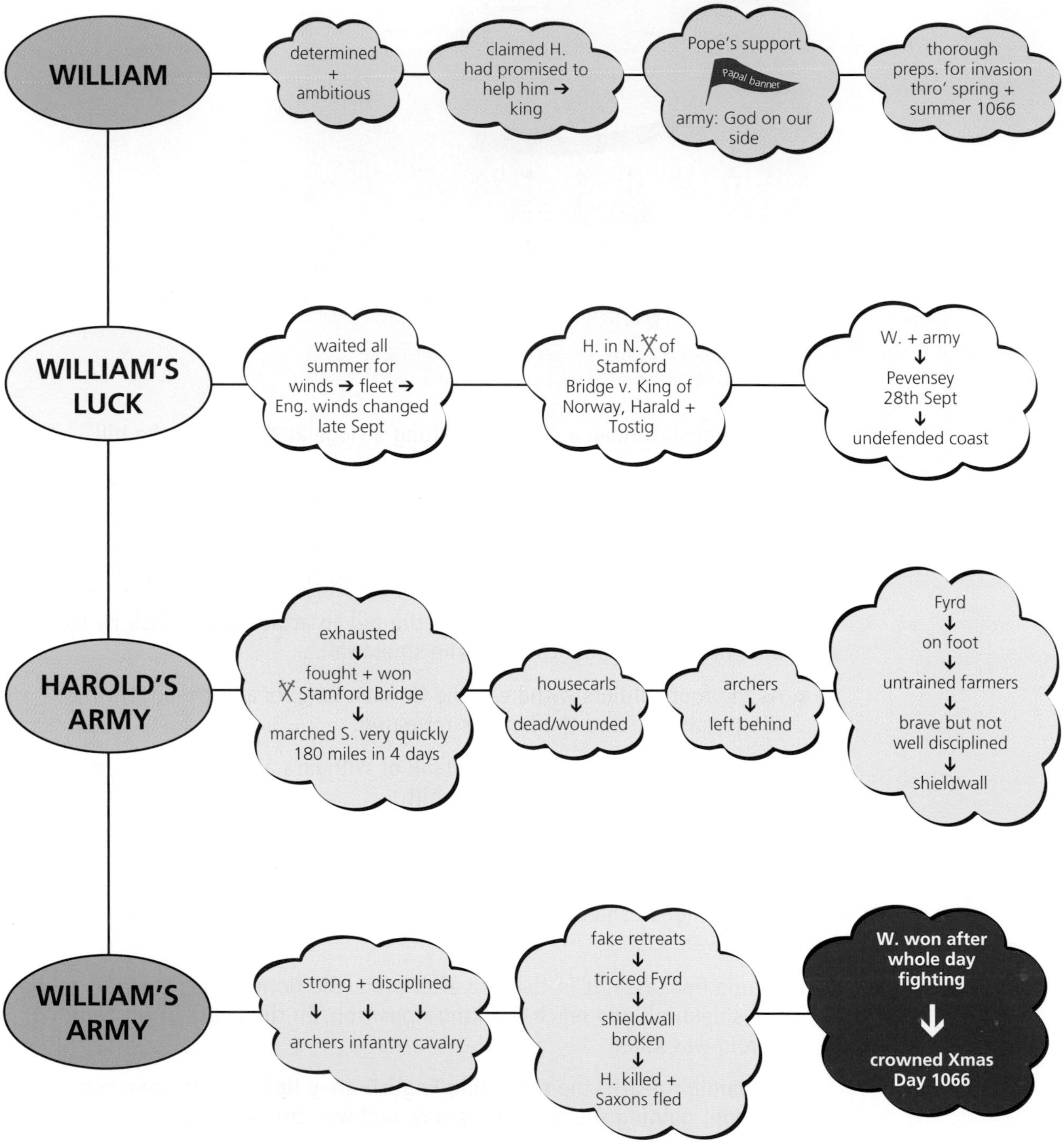

■ This flow chart is adapted from *Study Skills*, page 52.

Evidence question

You may be asked to answer an evidence question on the Norman Conquest. Refer to the guidance on page xi and make sure that you practise answering these questions.

★ Make sure you know

- ★ The three main claimants to the crown of England in 1066.
- ★ The preparations made by Harold and William before the invasion of England.
- ★ The events of the Battle of Stamford Bridge.
- ★ The events of the Battle of Hastings.

Test yourself

Before moving on to the next chapter, make sure you can answer the following questions. The answers are at the back of the book.

1 According to William, what did Harold do in 1052 that entitled the Duke to the throne of England?

____

2 Which member of Harold Godwinson's family supported Harald Hardrada?

____

3 What was the Witan?

____

4 When and where did the Normans land in England?

____

5 When and where was the battle fought between Harold and William?

____

2 Conquered England

William I needed to make sure that he could maintain control over the people, keeping them loyal to him and putting down any rebellions.

2.1 Medieval rule and the Feudal System

The Feudal System was a system of controlling the different levels of society and making sure that the King could raise an army when one was needed.

- The King owned all the land in the kingdom. He held some for himself to provide income for his household and government.
- The rest he gave to his tenants-in-chief, who were powerful barons and churchmen such as bishops. In return, the King expected them to be loyal to him.
- These tenants-in-chief demonstrated their loyalty by paying homage to the King. They knelt and solemnly swore fealty to him, becoming the King's vassal. They had to defend the King by providing soldiers from the lands they held.
- The tenants-in-chief gave some land to knights, who similarly paid homage to them and became their vassals.
- The knights also kept some land for themselves and gave the rest to freemen (or peasants), who made up the lowest level of the Feudal System.

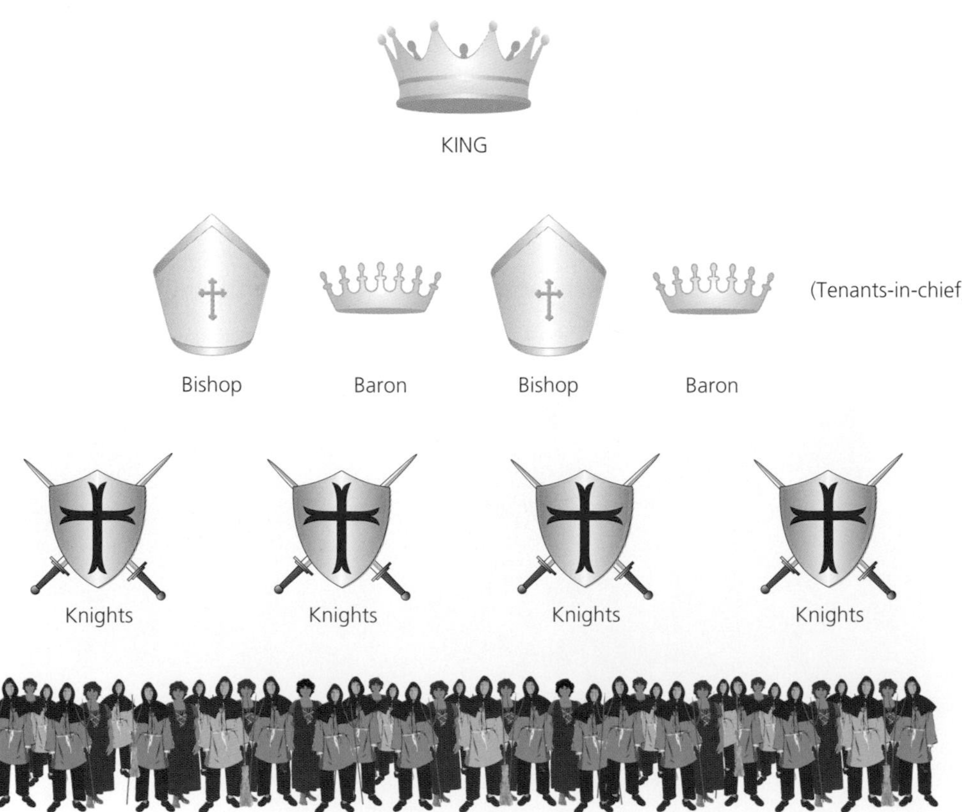

Revision tip

You could try making up a phrase to help you remember the order of the Feudal System:

King	Kevin
Tenants-in-chief	Took
Knights	Karen's
Freemen	Frisbee

2.2 Revolts and rebellions

William allowed some important Englishmen to keep their positions, as long as they swore fealty to him, but he soon regretted this decision.

- In 1069, the English earls Edwin of Mercia and Morcar of Northumbria rebelled with the help of some Vikings and Scots, taking the city of York.
- In revenge, William ordered that huge areas of Yorkshire be laid waste. This became known as the 'Harrying of the North'.
- Another English rebel, known as Hereward the Wake, operated in the marshlands of East Anglia. He has become a legendary figure with many stories told about him.

2.3 New buildings

In order to keep control over the people, the Normans introduced the castle to England.

- The first were motte and bailey castles. They were easy and quick to build, using local workers and materials. However, being wooden, they could be burnt down and would rot over time.

English people in important positions were gradually replaced by Normans. The new bishops began to rebuild churches in the Norman style, which typically used thick stone walls with rounded arches over the doors and windows.

2.4 The Domesday Book

The Domesday Book records the results of a nationwide survey ordered by William at Christmas 1085. Historians believe this was done for several reasons:

- A Viking invasion may have seemed likely. William wanted to know exactly how many soldiers he could recruit to defend his lands from the threat overseas.
- William may have suspected that some of his barons were holding land that should have belonged to him or the Church.
- William wanted to know where he could charge people more tax.

The Norman officials asked all the landholders for the following information:

- The name of the manor.
- The name of the landholder.
- The size of the land.
- How much belonged to the landholder.
- How many men worked on the land.
- How many amenities – such as mills or churches – were on the land.
- How much the land was worth.

Revision tip

You could use pictures to help you remember the questions that were asked. Think what you would draw for each of the table entries below; the first one has been done for you.

Manor name	
Landholder name	
Land size	
Land held by landholder	
Number of men	
Amenities	
Value	

So that William could get an idea as to how things had changed over time, the questions were asked with reference to three periods:

- During the reign of King Edward (before 1066).
- When King William granted the land to the landholder (shortly after 1066).
- At the current time (around 1086).

2.5 Life in the manor

The manor was the unit of land used for farming.

- Freemen tended to be the wealthiest class of peasant. They generally governed the people who did the manual work.
- Villeins, or serfs, held their own land from the freemen and worked on it themselves.
- Cottars did not hold any land to farm themselves, but instead were hired to work on other people's land.
- Each village had a church and the most important manors also had a manor house where the lord of the manor lived.

The peasants in England used a system known as open-field farming.

- The land in a village consisted of two or three large, open fields. These would be divided into long strips of land, which were held by the freemen and villeins.
- The strips belonging to the lord of the manor formed his demesne. This would be ploughed each year, either by villeins or cottars.
- One of the fields would be left fallow during the year. It would be ploughed but no crop would be planted on it.
- There was also a meadow for growing long grasses that could be used as hay for the animals. Woodland provided wood for buildings and fuel. Common land was for people to graze their animals on.
- All the peasants in the village harvested the whole crop as one. The harvested corn was threshed and the grain was divided among all the farmers.

Essay question

Try this sample essay question for yourself. A suggested answer is given at the back of the book.

Q Explain how William I dealt with opposition to his rule. (30)

★ Make sure you know

- ★ How the Feudal System worked.
- ★ The main English revolts against William and how he dealt with them.
- ★ The features of the new buildings the Normans introduced to England.
- ★ The reasons for, and information contained within, the Domesday Book.
- ★ The characteristics of an 11th-century manor.

Test yourself

Before moving on to the next chapter, make sure you can answer the following questions. The answers are at the back of the book.

1 If a landholder swore fealty in an act of homage, what did he become?

____

2 Which northern city did Edwin and Morcar re-take from the Normans?

____

3 What were the typical features of Norman churches?

____

4 What are the three periods of time referred to in the Domesday Book?

____

5 Which class of peasant was paid wages to work because they did not hold land themselves?

____

6 What was the name given to the land held by the lord of the manor?

____

3 The sons of William I

William I had three sons: Robert, William and Henry.

On his deathbed, he declared that Robert would become the Duke of Normandy and William the King of England.

3.1 William II (1087–1100)

William II was known as 'Rufus' (the Red) and he ruled England for thirteen years.

- He managed to crush rebellions, including one by his elder brother Robert, who believed that he should have been King of England.
- William believed that he ruled the Church in England, but Archbishop Anselm of Canterbury argued that the Pope was in charge. In 1097, Anselm left England in despair and William continued to take Church money and land.
- William II was killed in 1100; hit in the chest with an arrow while out hunting. His brother Henry quickly declared himself the new King of England.

3.2 Henry I (1100–1135)

Henry I was not a soldier, but he could be ruthless in getting what he wanted.

- Henry's brother Robert claimed once again to be the true King of England. The rebellion was put down and Robert was imprisoned for life.
- Henry's barons in France often started rebellions. All revolts were crushed, however, and Henry managed to hold on to Normandy.
- Henry encouraged monasteries to be built and appointed churchmen to important positions in government. He invited Anselm to return to England.
- But Henry and Anselm argued over who should appoint bishops and abbots. Anselm held his view that the Pope governed the whole Church. Henry felt that since these churchmen were often important government leaders and major landholders, he should choose them.
- A compromise was reached. The King would privately make his personal choice, then the Church would 'elect' this person officially.

3.3 Matilda

Henry had one legitimate son, named William, but in 1120 the young prince was drowned when his ship sank in the English Channel.

- Henry therefore wanted his daughter Matilda to become queen. His barons were very reluctant to agree because she was a woman.
- Henry arranged for Matilda to marry Geoffrey Plantagenet, hoping that Geoffrey would support her as queen.
- The barons were eventually persuaded to give Matilda their support.
- Geoffrey rebelled against the King and provoked Henry into fighting him in France. Henry died there in 1135.

Revision tip

Use a flow chart to help you remember what happened to Robert, William II, Henry I and Matilda. The title could be 'What happened to William I's heirs' and then have four rows, one for each of Robert, William, Henry and Matilda. Summarise the key points for each in separate bubbles. The chart below shows how you might start it.

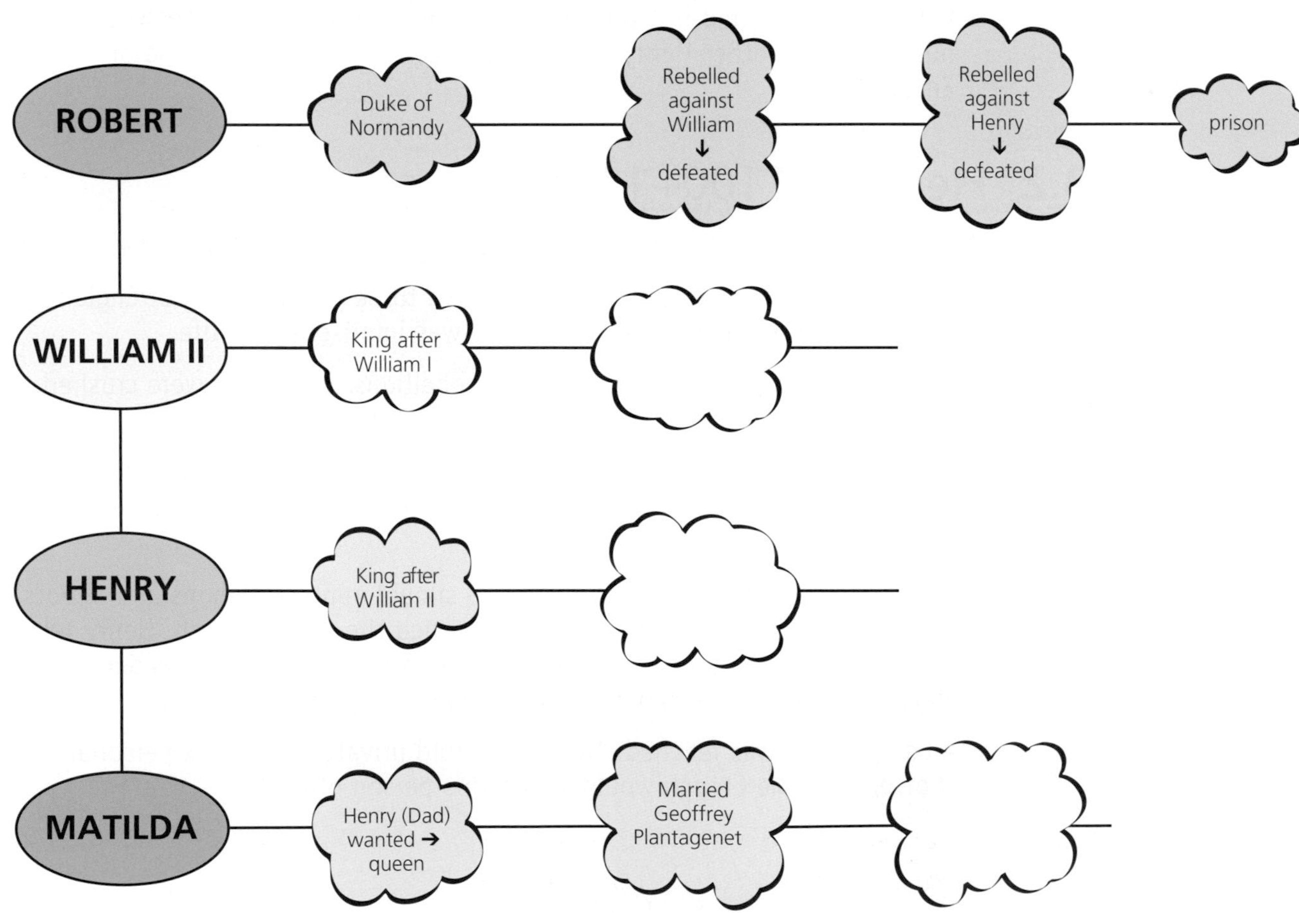

3.4 The Church

In the Middle Ages, the Church influenced every part of the life of every person.

- Priests preached that those who followed their religion would go to Heaven. Otherwise they would go to Hell. The people were reminded of Hell by murals painted on church walls.
- Mass was spoken in Latin, which only the educated could understand.
- The village priest would baptise babies, marry couples and bury the dead.
- A bishop was based in a cathedral. He was a significant landholder and was able to raise Church taxes called tithes.
- The bishops were controlled by the two archbishops of Canterbury and York. The Archbishop of Canterbury was the head of the Church in England.
- The head of the worldwide Church was the Pope, usually based in Rome.

3.5 Monasteries and nunneries

Some churchmen and women lived in monasteries and nunneries. Monks and nuns were supposed to follow the rules of their order, for example the order of St Benedict.

The three most important rules of St Benedict were:

- Obedience: following God's will, through the authority of the Church leaders.
- Poverty: not owning any earthly possessions.
- Chastity: not having relationships with the opposite sex, marrying or having children.

A typical day for a monk or a nun would be like this:

- Midnight: Matins, a church service lasting an hour.
- 6 am: Prime, another service, followed by breakfast and then work or study.
- 9 am: Chapter Mass, followed by a reading of the rules of the order in the chapter house and a discussion on how the monastery should be run.
- 11 am: High Mass.
- Noon: Lunch and an afternoon nap.
- 2 pm: Nones, another service, followed by work.
- 4 pm: Vespers, an evening service, followed by more work.
- 6 pm: Supper.
- 7 pm: Compline, the final service of the day, then bed.

Revision tip

You could try using an index card to help you remember the typical day of a monk. Put the times on the front of the card and your answers on the back. To see how to produce index cards, see *Study Skills*, pages 54–58. Or, to remember the names of the services, why not try a mnemonic – try making up one of your own or use the one below.

Many **p**eople **c**hoose to **h**ave **l**unch; Matins, Prime, Chapter, High, Lunch;

No one **v**olunteers for **s**upper **c**ompletely! Nones, Vespers, Supper, Compline.

Monks and nuns often had a vital role to play in society.

- They provided education for youngsters who joined the order. Monasteries had large libraries full of books, which the monks would make copies of.
- Monasteries gave food to the poor and shelter to travellers. Often, local people would be employed as servants.
- If the monastery became too wealthy, the rules of St Benedict were sometimes forgotten and some monks began to live with more luxuries. Local people gave gifts of money because they believed that this would secure them a place in Heaven.

Essay question

Try this sample essay question for yourself. A suggested answer is given at the back of the book.

Q Explain the significance of the Church on life in England in the Middle Ages. (30)

★ Make sure you know

- ★ The strengths and weaknesses of William II and the events of his reign.
- ★ The strengths and weaknesses of Henry I and the events of his reign.
- ★ The position of Henry's daughter Matilda.
- ★ The features of the Church and its influence on the lives of ordinary people.
- ★ The rules and daily life in the monasteries and nunneries.

Test yourself

Before moving on to the next chapter, make sure you can answer the following questions. The answers are at the back of the book.

1 Which famous churchman quarrelled with William II?

2 Why did Henry I face such a dilemma over who should succeed him?

3 Why were church walls decorated with murals?

4 How might increased wealth lead to a monastery not following the rules of St Benedict?

From civil war to Henry II

4.1 Stephen (1135–54)

When Henry died in 1135, Stephen, the Count of Blois, rushed to England and claimed the throne for himself.

- Stephen was the grandson of William the Conqueror.
- Henry's daughter, Matilda, sailed from France in 1139 and began to raise an army. However, when she marched on London, the people turned against her and Matilda was driven out of the city.
- The civil war lasted for fourteen years. This period has become known as the Anarchy. The *Anglo-Saxon Chronicle* describes it as a period when *'Christ and his saints slept'*.
- Matilda left England in 1153 and her son Henry, the Duke of Normandy, continued the struggle on her behalf. He and Stephen agreed that Henry would take over the throne of England when Stephen died.

Revision tip

You could make up a story that connects the facts of what happened once Henry I died, up until Henry II became King (see *Study Skills*, page 66). Ask someone to read the story back to you so that you can visualise the story unfolding in your head.

4.2 Henry II (1154–89)

Henry II continued the work of his grandfather, Henry I, by increasing royal justice.

- He encouraged the growth of assizes. The assizes took power away from the barons' courts and this meant any fines obtained went directly to the King.
- Before the legal reforms, trials were often settled by ordeal.

4.3 Thomas Becket

Henry II's Royal Chancellor was Thomas Becket. Henry wanted Becket to take over when the Archbishop of Canterbury died, as he was keen to have an ally who would allow him to control the Church.

- Henry and Becket argued over the issue of criminous clerks. Henry wanted them to face trial in royal courts, meaning that any fines would come to the King.
- In 1164, the Constitutions of Clarendon stated that no one could be excommunicated without the King's permission; no churchman could leave England without the King's permission; and criminous clerks would be sentenced by the royal courts. Becket refused to accept these rules.

- Becket fled to France and Henry seized his lands. In the meantime, Henry decided to crown his son King of England in order that Henry could concentrate on his lands in France. When he attempted to use Archbishop Roger of York for the coronation, the Pope objected. Henry was forced to make peace with Becket in 1170.
- Becket excommunicated everyone who had been involved in the Prince's coronation. Outraged, the King is said to have shouted: *'Will no one rid me of this turbulent priest?'*
- On 29 December 1170, four knights rushed into Canterbury Cathedral and declared Becket a traitor. The knights set upon him with their swords and killed him.
- Henry was blamed for Becket's death. In penance, Henry prayed at Becket's tomb and walked through Canterbury allowing himself to be whipped.

Revision tip

Try using a flow chart to show the rise and fall of Thomas Becket. Use pictures instead of words in the chart, for example the King and Becket arguing, Becket fleeing to France by boat, the knights killing Becket with their swords. It doesn't matter if you can't draw very well – use 'stick men' for the people and use different colours or captions to show who is who. The one below has been started for you.

Rise and fall of Thomas Becket

Evidence question

You may be asked to answer an evidence question on Archbishop Becket. Refer to the guidance on page xi and make sure that you practise answering these questions.

4.4 Eleanor of Aquitaine and the sons of Henry II

Henry II's marriage to Eleanor of Aquitaine allowed the King to rule over most of France, and he spent most of his reign there.

- Eleanor of Aquitaine had a strong and dominant personality. She had been married to King Louis VII of France, but the marriage was annulled in 1152 and Eleanor married Henry two months later.
- Henry and Eleanor had four sons: Henry, Richard, Geoffrey and John. The King often trusted Eleanor to look after his kingdom in England. Soon Eleanor began to side with her sons and against their father.

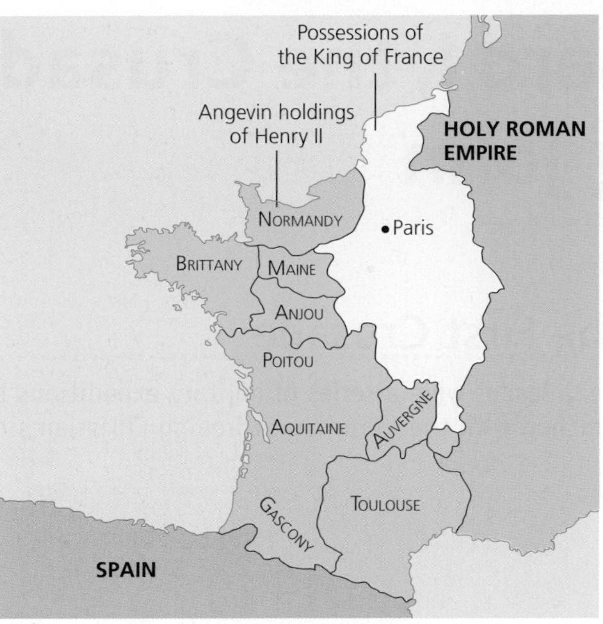

■ Medieval France and the Angevin holdings

- The four brothers were impatient for power and quarrelled with their father. In 1173, encouraged by their mother, Princes Henry, Richard and Geoffrey rebelled against the King.
- Eleanor was imprisoned for the rest of the King's life. Henry spent two years trying to defeat the uprisings. Henry and Geoffrey died before their father, and Richard and John rebelled again in 1188 with the help of the King of France. Henry II died the following year.

★ Make sure you know

★ The reasons for the civil war between Stephen and Matilda.

★ The work of Henry II in improving royal justice.

★ The struggle between the King and the Church that led to the murder of Thomas Becket.

★ The problems caused by Eleanor of Aquitaine and the four sons of Henry II.

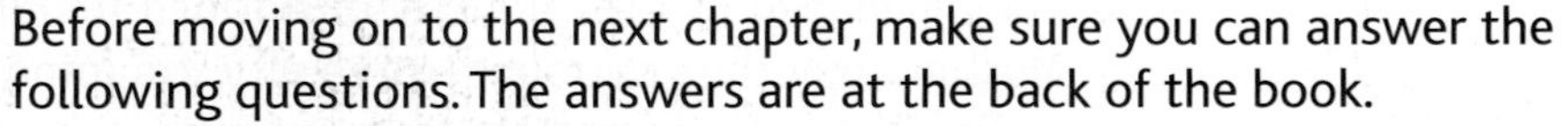

Test yourself

Before moving on to the next chapter, make sure you can answer the following questions. The answers are at the back of the book.

1 Which three points of the Constitutions of Clarendon did Becket refuse to accept?

2 What event caused the Pope to object to Henry II's dealings with the Church?

3 Name four key people involved in the 1173 rebellion against Henry II.

5 Richard I, the Crusades and King John

5.1 The First Crusade

The Crusades were a series of military expeditions to the Holy Land. They were launched with the intention of freeing Christian sites from Muslim control.

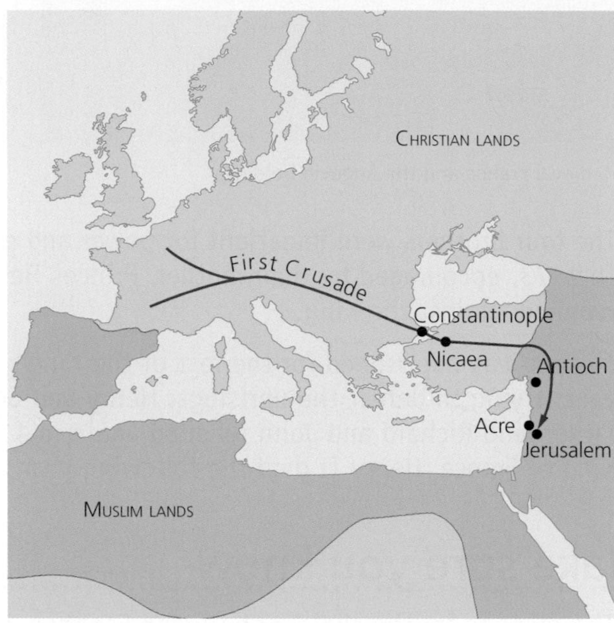

■ The Holy Land and the route of the First Crusade

- Pope Urban II launched the First Crusade in 1095 to free the city of Jerusalem from the Muslims.
- Thousands of people made the 2,000-mile march to the Holy Land. However, they were undisciplined fighters and many were slaughtered by Muslim forces.
- A second wave of crusaders was led by nobles such as Robert of Normandy and Stephen of Blois.
- They managed to take the city of Antioch in June 1098. However, the Muslim army then surrounded the city, trapping the crusaders within the walls. They were forced to leave the city.
- The crusaders took Jerusalem a year later. The lands they controlled across the Holy Land were divided up into crusader states.
- The Second Crusade was launched in 1145 and was led by Louis VII of France – accompanied by his wife Eleanor of Aquitaine (see page 18). This army intended to reinforce the Christian soldiers in Jerusalem, but was forced to turn back in 1148 after a failed siege of the city of Damascus.

? **Evidence question**

You may be asked to answer an evidence question on the First Crusade. Refer to the guidance on page xi and make sure that you practise answering these questions.

5.2 Richard I (1189–99) and the Third Crusade

Richard I was devout, strong and courageous – earning the nickname 'Lionheart'. He travelled so much that he only spent six months of his ten-year reign in England.

- Richard and Philip II of France decided to lead a crusade in 1191.
- Richard arrived at Acre to find Philip's army of crusaders besieging the city, while surrounded by a Muslim army led by the commander Saladin. Acre eventually surrendered in July 1191 and a truce with Saladin was agreed.
- When the sick Philip returned to France, Richard was left in charge of the whole Crusade. He believed that Saladin was not keeping the agreed truce and ordered several thousand Muslim prisoners to be openly massacred in front of Saladin's army.
- The crusaders marched south, taking the city of Jaffa. Richard began to receive reports that his old ally Philip of France was preparing to take his French lands from him. Despite the best efforts of the crusaders, Saladin's forces still managed to hold Jerusalem.
- The Muslims then attempted to retake Jaffa from the crusaders. A stalemate was reached: with Saladin constantly attacking Jaffa, Richard was forced to defend the city and could not carry on to Jerusalem.
- The crusaders grew weary and ill, and eventually Saladin and Richard agreed a truce. Richard could keep all the land he had conquered down to Jaffa, but everything south of the city, including Jerusalem, had to be left for Saladin.

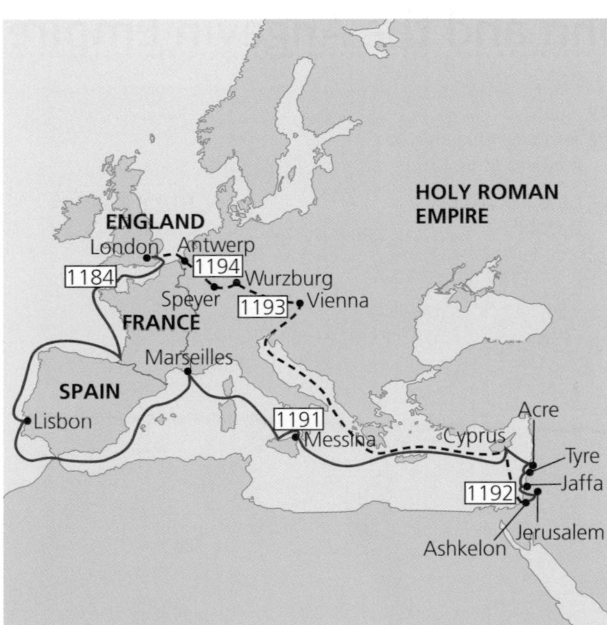

■ The route of the Third Crusade

Richard left the Holy Land in October 1192. He soon found that many of his enemies had been plotting against him.

- Richard attempted to travel back through Austria and Germany. He was captured near Vienna and handed over to the Emperor of Germany, who demanded a ransom of 100,000 marks for his release. It took two years for the money to be raised, leaving England nearly bankrupt. Richard was set free in 1194.

- Philip of France had been plotting with Richard's brother John to take control of Normandy. Richard arrived in England and put down John's rebellion. He then spent the next four years in France fighting Philip, managing to reclaim most of the land that Philip had taken.
- In 1199, Richard was killed, almost by accident, when he was hit by a stray crossbow bolt. On his deathbed, Richard forgave his brother John and declared him to be his successor as King of England.

Revision tip

Index cards could be a good way of remembering the sequence of events for the crusades. Use one card for each crusade. Think up questions for the fronts of the cards and write your answers on the back. For example, the card for the First Crusade might have the following questions on the front:

First wave:
Who?
When?
Where?
Second wave:
Who?
When?
Where?

Then test yourself by seeing if you can answer the questions.

5.3 John and the Angevin Empire

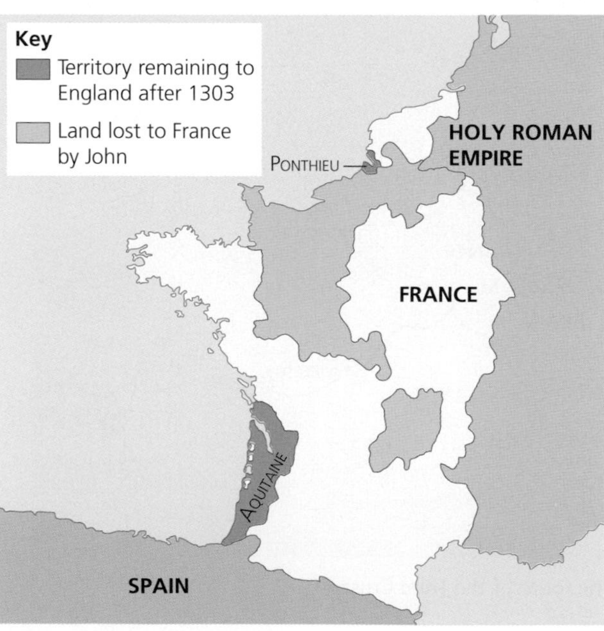

■ King John's holdings in France

John was known as 'Lackland' because, as his father's youngest son, he should not have inherited any land. As it turned out, he inherited both England and vast lands in France. But he was not very successful in keeping hold of it.

- Philip II of France now turned against John. He claimed that John's nephew Arthur – the son of his brother Geoffrey – had a better claim to the English throne and the Angevin lands (see the family tree on page 188). John captured and imprisoned his nephew, and agreed a treaty with him that made Philip respect his right to the throne.
- In 1200, John married Isabella of Angoulême, who had been betrothed to Hugh Lusignan. This annoyed the Lusignan family, who complained to Philip, who attacked John's French lands.
- John's nephew Arthur went missing in 1203, fuelling rumours that the King had had him murdered. John's mother Eleanor of Aquitaine died the following year. She had been well respected and after her death many barons refused to continue supporting her son. Normandy fell to Philip in 1204, followed by most of John's remaining land in France.
- John reintroduced a tax called scutage that was only supposed to be used in times of war.

5.4 John and the Church

John believed that he alone had the right to control the Church in England. When the Archbishop of Canterbury died in 1205, John wanted to choose his successor.

- Pope Innocent III nominated the scholar Stephen Langton to be the new Archbishop. When John refused to accept Langton, the Pope placed England under an interdict in 1208.
- John was excommunicated in 1209 but would still not give in. He only backed down in 1213, when the Pope started to encourage Philip II to invade England. This was too much of a risk for John to take. He agreed to accept Langton as Archbishop and swore fealty to the Pope.

5.5 Magna Carta

John now prepared to take his lands back from Philip II. But his plans fell apart and John was forced to agree a humiliating peace with the French King.

- This was the last straw for the nobles in England. When John refused to meet them to discuss matters, some barons raised an army against the King and marched to London in May 1215.
- John was forced to meet the rebel barons at Runnymede, near Windsor. There, the barons presented the King with the Magna Carta ('great charter'), listing their demands.

The Magna Carta was intended to restrict the powers of the King. Some of the 63 clauses still have consequences today:

- The King was to leave the Church to govern itself.
- The King could not raise taxes without the agreement of his nobles.
- The level at which the King could set certain taxes was restricted.
- Freemen were entitled to a fair trial and could not be fined, imprisoned or otherwise punished without one.
- Any punishment should be fair and fit the crime.

6.2 Edward I (1272–1307)

By the time he came to the throne in 1272, Edward I had a reputation as a fine military leader.

- Edward tended to use Parliament to his benefit. He passed the Statute of Gloucester, which gave more power to the royal courts, and the Statute of Mortmain, which restricted the amount of land that could be given to the Church.
- However, Edward still believed that he could ignore Parliament's will on some matters. Knowing that a tax raise would need the approval of Parliament, he tried to raise money in other ways. For example, in 1290, he drove all the Jews out of England and confiscated their property.

6.3 Wales and Scotland

Edward I had an ambition to unite all parts of the British Isles under his leadership. He wanted the monarchs in Wales and Scotland to pay him homage.

The Welsh campaign

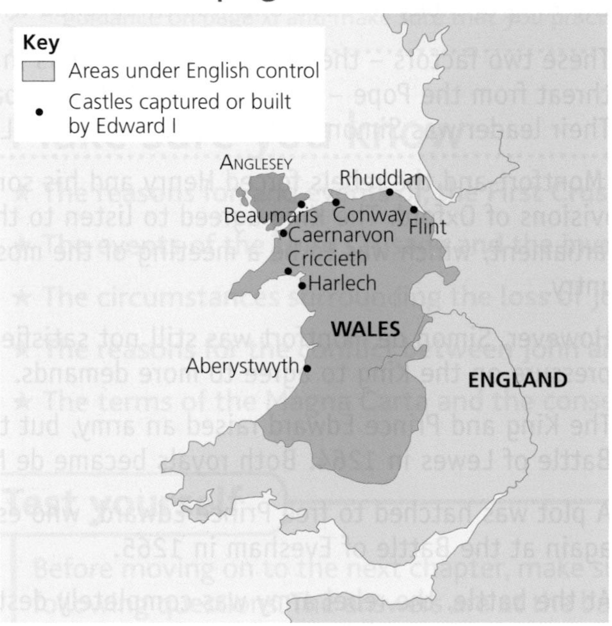

■ Wales at the time of Edward I

- Prince Llewelyn of Wales refused to pay homage to Edward. In retaliation, Edward sent three English armies into Wales in 1276–77.
- The Welsh fought in mountainous areas such as Snowdonia. The English managed to cut them off from the island of Anglesey, where the Welsh obtained food supplies, and forced Llewelyn's men to surrender. Edward forced Llewelyn to pay him homage.
- Llewelyn and his brother David fought back in 1282, taking several English castles. Edward invaded Wales, using the same trick of cutting off Anglesey. Llewelyn was killed and David sentenced to be hanged, drawn and quartered as a traitor.

- Edward built a string of castles around the coastline that were stronger than any seen before (see pages 33–34). English law was introduced to Wales, and more and more English people began to settle there.

The Scottish campaign

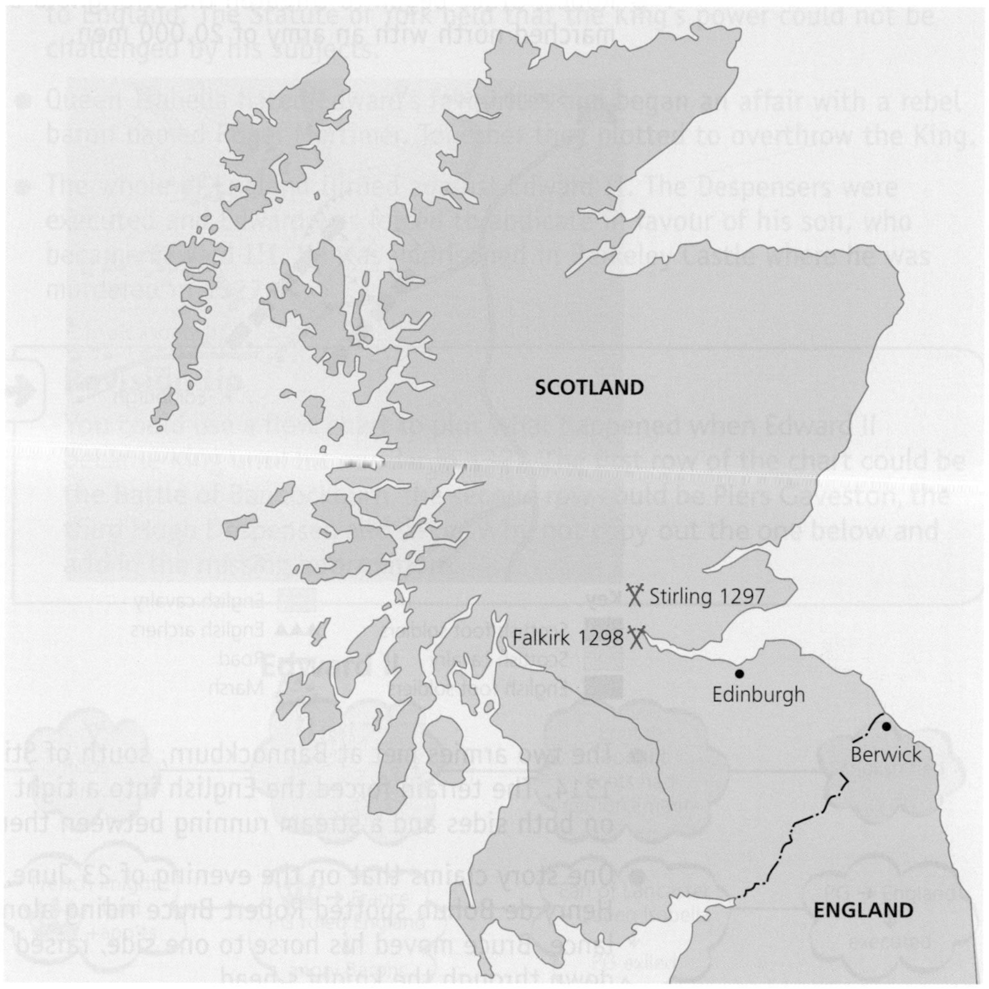

- When Queen Margaret of Scotland died in 1290, she had no clear successor. The Scottish nobles nominated the three best candidates – John Balliol, Robert Bruce and John Hastings – and asked Edward to choose who should be king.
- Edward chose John Balliol, who was crowned King John of Scotland in 1292. But in 1295, John made an alliance with the King of France, who had seized Gascony from the English. Edward then invaded Scotland and took over John's kingdom.
- William Wallace gathered an army to fight against the English. He was victorious at the Battle of Stirling Bridge in 1297, but beaten at Falkirk the following year. He was eventually captured in 1305 and executed.
- Robert Bruce began to lead the Scottish rebels in 1306. Edward prepared another invasion of Scotland but died in northern England in 1307.

The 1346 campaign

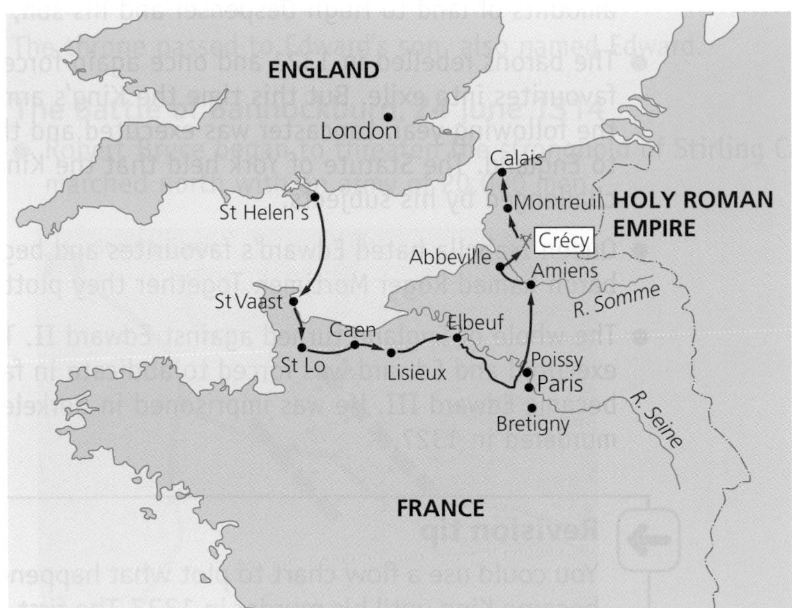

- In July 1346, Edward and 15,000 English soldiers sailed to Normandy. They headed east, looting and destroying the coastal towns.
- When they reached the River Seine, the English found that the French army had destroyed all the bridges. They were forced to march south-east towards Paris. At Poissy they managed to rebuild the bridge and cross safely.
- The French managed to reach the River Somme first and destroyed or guarded all the bridges. The English marched north-west and forced their way across the river at Blanchetaque, near Abbeville – straight into the path of Philip VI's army.

6.7 The Battle of Crécy, 26 August 1346

The two armies met in a field near the village of Crécy on the evening of 26 August 1346.

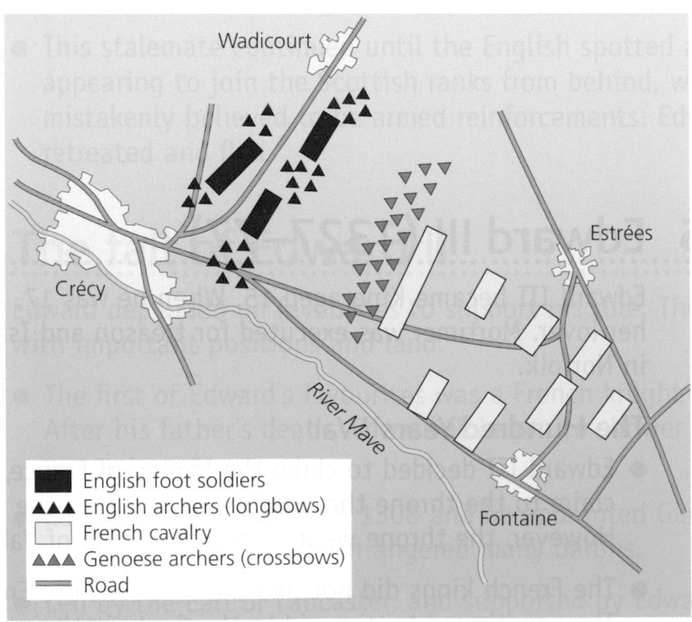

- The English army, made up of 12,000 foot soldiers, lined up on a ridge facing south-east. They stood in two large groups, commanded by the Earl of Northampton and Edward, Prince of Wales, nicknamed 'the Black Prince'. King Edward commanded a smaller group behind the main two.
- The French army, made up of between 30,000 and 40,000 men, stood in the valley below the ridge. They consisted mostly of mounted knights, with a long line of Genoese archers at the front.
- The English longbowmen fired constant barrages of arrows down onto the Genoese, who began to retreat.
- The French made several charges up to the ridge and at one point managed to reach Prince Edward's position. When a message reached King Edward that the Prince needed help he dismissed it, saying that he wanted his son to 'earn his spurs'.
- Eventually the French horses and knights were exhausted and they retreated, having lost 10,000 men.

Edward then marched towards Calais, believing he could take the town easily.

- Calais was strongly fortified and Edward was forced to besiege the town. The siege lasted a year, but eventually the people of Calais surrendered.
- The French inhabitants were driven out of the city and replaced by English settlers.

6.8 The last years of Edward III

- The Black Death reached Europe in 1348, causing hostilities to pause for a few years. Edward was confident in placing command with his son, the 'Black Prince', who was largely successful in France.
- In England, there were protests about the heavy taxation needed to fund the war. Edward eventually allowed Parliament more control over taxation.
- In 1376, Parliament began to demand further reforms. In a session that became known as the Good Parliament, the barons demanded that the King's advisors be removed before any more money could be raised.
- By the following year, Edward's son John of Gaunt had used his strong influence to return many of the advisors to their positions.

Edward III died in 1377, having had four sons from his marriage to Philippa of Hainault (see the family trees on pages 189 and 190).

- The eldest son, 'the Black Prince', had died before his father, in 1376. On his deathbed, he had made his father and brother, John of Gaunt, swear that they would recognise his son Richard as the heir to the throne. At the time of the King's death the following year, Richard was just nine years old.

★ Make sure you know

- ★ The causes and events of the conflict between Henry III, Simon de Montfort and an emerging Parliament.
- ★ The personality of Edward I and the events of his campaigns against Wales and Scotland.
- ★ The details of the Battle of Bannockburn and the reasons for the overthrowing of Edward II.
- ★ The events of the Hundred Years' War, including the 1346 campaign and the Battle of Crécy.
- ★ The position of Edward III in England during his final years.

Test yourself

Before moving on to the next chapter, make sure you can answer the following questions. The answers are at the back of the book.

1 At which battle was Simon de Montfort killed?

2 Which trick did Edward I twice use to defeat Llewelyn of Wales?

3 Who won the Battle of Stirling Bridge in 1297?

4 Why did the English retreat hurriedly from the battlefield at Bannockburn?

5 Which rebel baron plotted with Queen Isabella to overthrow Edward II?

7 Life in the Middle Ages

7.1 Castles

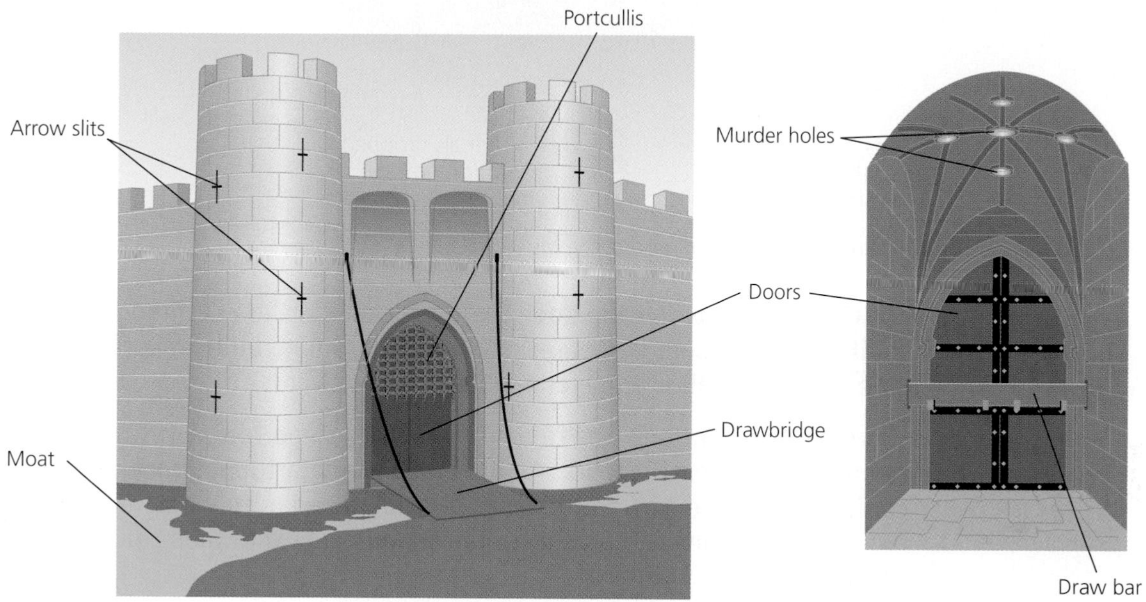

- The Normans brought the motte and bailey castle to Britain (see page 9). They could be constructed quickly, using local materials and labour. But, being wooden, they could be burnt and were susceptible to rot. Most did not last more than twenty years.
- Some motte and bailey castles were rebuilt as stone buildings. The wall around the bailey could become a curtain wall, and a shell keep or tower keep could be built on top of the motte to replace the wooden building.
- Medieval armies used siege warfare and the castles needed to withstand constant attempts to breach the walls. Many castles were surrounded by a moat. Over the moat was a drawbridge, which could be raised to prevent entry. In front of the main door was a portcullis, which could be dropped down, and a draw bar could be pulled across.

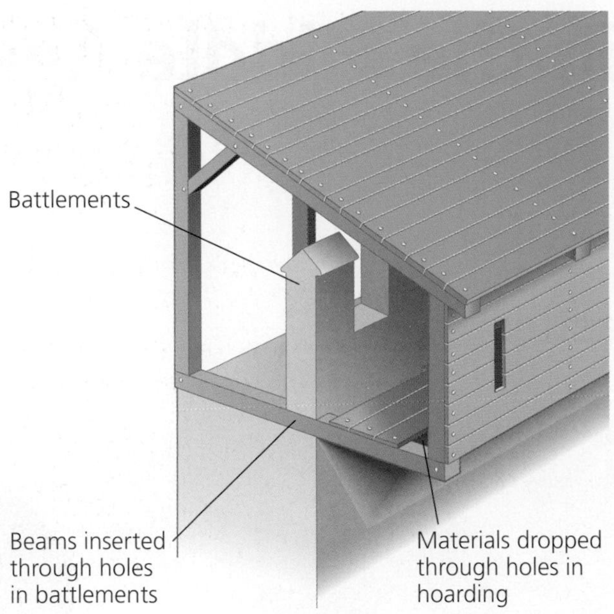

■ Hoardings: defences to protect the castle walls

- In the ceiling behind the door there were murder holes, through which boiling liquid could be poured. Wooden hoardings, built over the tops of the walls, also allowed defenders to fire downwards.
- One method of attack was to use a belfry, or siege tower, so that men could climb over the battlements. Another was to dig a tunnel underneath the wall, causing the wall to collapse. Defenders began to build round towers, which were stronger than square ones, and made the walls thicker at the bottom.

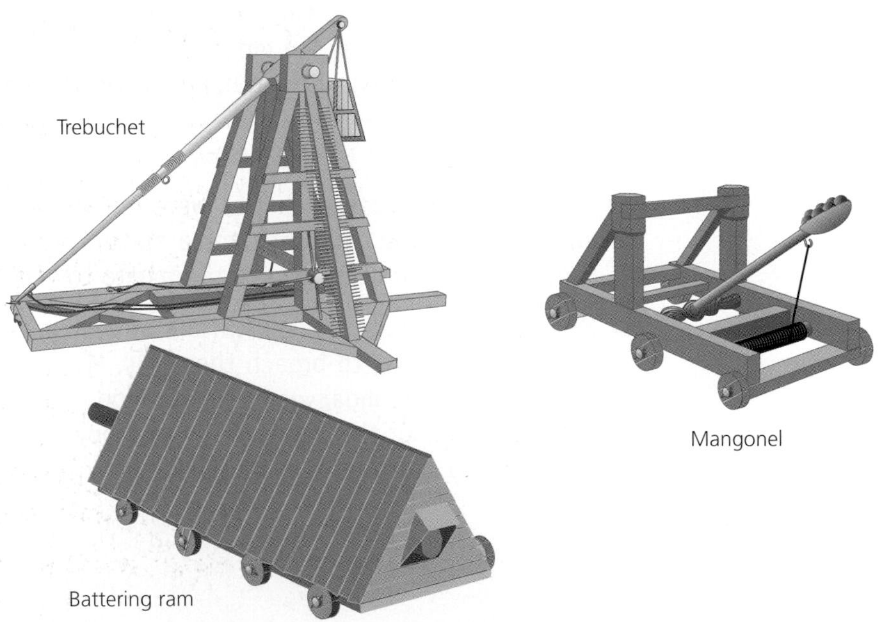

- A battering ram could weaken a wall if there was no moat or slope. Stone-throwing machines, such as mangonels or trebuchets, had advantages as they could be used from a distance.
- The attackers could simply surround the castle and wait until the defenders' food and supplies ran out. Sometimes this could take months or even years.
- Edward I built a series of very strong castles in Wales (see page 27). These had a circle of defences surrounded by another and so are known as concentric castles.

Castles were also homes for rich nobles and their families, and the grandest ones were built to display the great wealth of the owner.

- There was usually a great hall, in which the family met and dined. The family slept in a smaller, private room called a solar. The most important people lived on the higher floors, and the servants and soldiers down below.
- A cellar held all the supplies, which were plentiful in case of a siege, and the castle had its own well to provide water.
- By the 1500s, people were building houses for comfort rather than defence. Castles began to be replaced by large country houses.

7.2 The Jews

- Jewish settlers in medieval Britain were mostly in the business of money lending. They were tolerated by kings and nobles, who often needed to borrow from them.
- Towards the end of the twelfth century, Jews began to be subject to attacks called pogroms.
- The anti-Jewish feeling was stirred up by false stories about them. The stories, known today as blood libel, told of Jews kidnapping and murdering Christian children.
- By the thirteenth century, the government was passing anti-Jewish laws. Jews were not allowed to eat with Christians, or go out at Easter, and were made to wear yellow cloth in public. In 1275, they were banned from lending money, which deprived most Jews of their livelihood.
- In 1290, a law introduced by Edward I threw the Jews out of Britain altogether.

Revision tip

Try using pictures to help you remember all the main points about Jews at the time. You could either put these in a table with the key words in the left-hand column and your pictures in the right-hand column, or draw a sketch that includes all the different elements. Think what other illustrations you could use for the table below.

Money lenders	£
Pogroms	
Blood libel	
Anti-Jewish laws	
Out of Britain	

7.3 Medieval women

- In the Middle Ages, women were expected to work as hard as the men. They had to help their husbands work in the fields, cutting hay and corn and looking after the animals, and had to make produce such as cheese and butter, and then sell it at market. Some women took on extra work brewing ale or baking bread. They were expected to declare to their husbands any extra income they earned.
- Some women ran successful businesses in their own right. An example is Margery Kempe, who made a fortune brewing ale in King's Lynn, Norfolk. Another educated woman, also from Norfolk, was Margaret Paston, who was forced to take care of her husband's business while he was away.
- Upper-class women whose husbands held powerful positions were sometimes able to influence history in important ways. We know of Matilda, whose struggle to be recognised as queen caused a civil war with her cousin, and Eleanor of Aquitaine and Isabella of France, who both contributed significantly to the downfall of their husbands.

7.4 Medieval health and the Black Death

Doctors in the Middle Ages relied on the works of ancient Greek and Roman doctors, such as Galen, whose writings were largely out of date.

- Remedies for illnesses were based on superstition and were often dangerous. Patients were cut and left to bleed in the hope that the infection would escape. Later on, leeches were used to suck the blood from the body.
- It was believed that diseases were carried by smells in the air and were a punishment from God for disobedience.
- These false beliefs meant that proper prevention was impossible. Towns had poor sanitation, with no running water or drainage. The average person only lived for 40 years, with most deaths occurring during childhood. Childbirth often resulted in the mother's death.

The Black Death, a disease that originated in Asia, spread throughout Europe and reached Britain in 1348.

- Bubonic plague (caused by the bacteria *Yersinia pestis*) caused a bubo – a large swollen lymph gland – to appear in the armpit or groin. The victim usually died within five days.
- The plague arrived in Britain in June 1348, carried on two ships which landed at Melcombe in Dorset.
- Despite various attempts to stop the advance of disease, the people were powerless. The sick were abandoned and city gates were closed to strangers who might have brought the plague inside the walls. Flowers and herbs were used to purify the air, and fires were lit.
- The Black Death affected the Church terribly. Priests caught the disease themselves through contact with the sick. A group of people called flagellants, who believed that by whipping themselves they could persuade God to lift the punishment, were unsuccessful.

Revision tip

Make up a story that describes the spread of the Black Death, how it affected the people of Britain and what people did to try to stop it. Imagine the story in your head: see it as a film being played back as you think of the people who died and the flagellants whipping themselves to try to rid the country of the disease.

It is believed that at least a third of England's population was wiped out by the Black Death. As a result, the country lacked workers and resources.

- Surviving workers found themselves in demand and the lords who employed them had to pay much more for their services. Parliament passed the Statute of Labourers in 1351, which stated that all peasants had to work at the same rate as they had done in 1348. But many lords were forced to provide better working conditions and pay higher wages. The price of food increased because it was costing more to produce.

Evidence question

You may be asked to answer an evidence question on the Black Death. Refer to the guidance on page xi and make sure that you practise answering these questions.

★ Make sure you know

★ The layout and facilities of a typical medieval castle.

★ The position of Jews during the Middle Ages.

★ The position of women during the Middle Ages.

★ The causes, events and consequences of the Black Death in Britain.

Test yourself

Before moving on to the next chapter, make sure you can answer the following questions. The answers are at the back of the book.

1 What was the notable design feature of Edward I's castles in Wales?

____

2 What is the name for an anti-Jewish attack?

____

3 Which Norfolk woman handled her husband's business during his absence?

____

4 What is the name of the bacteria that causes bubonic plague?

____

5 Who were flagellants and what did they attempt to do?

____

8 Richard II and life in the towns

8.1 Richard II (1377–99) and the Peasants' Revolt

As his father had died the year before, Richard II inherited the throne in 1377 from his grandfather Edward III. He was placed into the care of his powerful uncle, John of Gaunt.

- Richard faced a serious crisis in 1381, when the villeins began to cause unrest in the countryside.
- The government introduced a Poll Tax in 1377. This was raised in 1379 and again in 1381, when it was trebled to one shilling, payable by everyone over the age of fourteen. It was almost impossible for peasants to afford this and they rose up against the government agents who had been sent to collect the money.
- The uprising spread throughout the south-east of England. Rebel leaders appeared, such as Wat Tyler in Kent. In June 1381, the rebels marched on London and demanded to speak to the King.
- Richard agreed to meet the rebels at Mile End on 14 June. He promised that people would in future be fairly paid and that nobody would be punished for the revolt. However, some of the rebels managed to break into the Tower of London and execute the Archbishop of Canterbury and the King's Treasurer.
- Richard again agreed to meet the rebels at Smithfield on 15 June. A supporter of the King insulted Wat Tyler and in the scuffle that followed the rebel leader was killed.
- Richard took control, calling out to the rebels that he was their true leader, and telling them to go home. Richard did not keep his promises and the other rebel leaders were captured and executed.

Revision tip

A flow chart could be a useful tool to help you remember the sequence of events of the Peasants' Revolt. Pick out the key words from each bullet point and, where possible, use pictures in your bubbles for these words.

Essay question

Try this sample essay question for yourself. A suggested answer is given at the back of the book.

Q Explain the significance of the Peasants' Revolt. (30)

8.2 The fall of Richard II

Richard II had handled the Peasants' Revolt well but soon became over-confident. He resented being under the control of his uncle John of Gaunt and tried to force Parliament to increase his powers.

- Parliament resisted and in the Merciless Parliament of 1388 the nobles demanded the arrest of Richard's supporters. The Lords Appellant took control of the government away from the King.
- In 1389, power was returned to Richard, who took several steps to increase his authority. He formed a permanent guard of personal knights and increased taxes, without the approval of Parliament.
- In 1397, Richard took his revenge on the Lords Appellant. One was executed, another murdered and the other three were sent into exile. One of these exiled lords was Henry Bolingbroke, the son of Richard's uncle, John of Gaunt.
- In February 1399, John of Gaunt died and Richard seized his uncle's lands instead of allowing them to go to Henry Bolingbroke. Bolingbroke came to England in June, gathered support from the nobles and arrested the King.
- Richard was deposed by Parliament in September 1399 and imprisoned in the Tower of London. Bolingbroke was crowned King Henry IV the following month. Richard was taken to Pontefract Castle, where he was murdered in February 1400.

8.3 Towns

While most people still lived in the countryside, the medieval period saw great growth in towns.

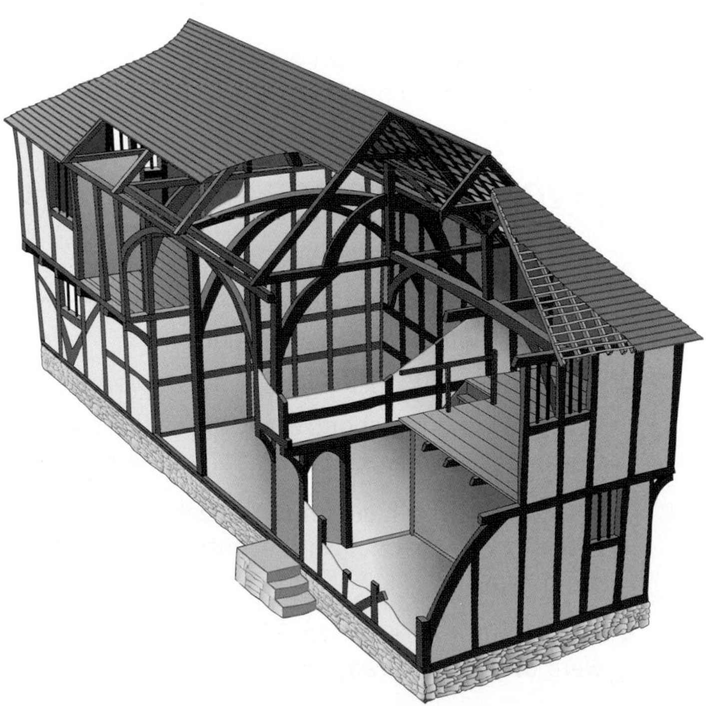

■ The structure of a medieval town house

- Buildings were made from a timber frame, with walls made with wattle and daub. The roofs were either thatched with straw or tiled.

- The streets were laid out so that there were several areas of common land for animals to graze and a large open area which was used as a marketplace for traders.
- Nearby would be a church or churches, and often a monastery or nunnery.
- Towns housed large groups of beggars, who targeted the wealthy tradesmen who lived in the towns to be close to their businesses.
- Boys who wanted to learn a trade for themselves first became apprentices, who were attached to a master craftsman by an agreement called an indenture. The master craftsmen taught them their trade and had to feed and clothe them. They would receive their labour and a sum of money from their families in return. Once the apprentices finished their training, they became journeymen and were able to work for their own wages.

8.4 Guilds

The tradesmen and craftsmen of a town sometimes formed an organisation together called a guild.

The idea of a guild was that the tradesmen and craftsmen would work together to protect each other's trade.

- Each guild had its own rules regarding who could set up business in their trade, the quality of the goods traded and the number of apprentices to be trained.
- Dishonest tradesmen who broke the rules of the guild were punished, usually by humiliation in front of the town. The usual way of doing this was to place the accused in a pillory or the stocks.
- The most important guildsmen had the chance to become mayor of the town and represent all the citizens. The wealthiest guilds were able to build guildhalls in which to meet.
- Guilds also put on town events such as pageants, mystery plays for entertainment and miracle plays, which had a religious message.

8.5 Town government, law and order

- Towns began to be granted charters by their lord or the King, which allowed the townspeople to form their own town government, and produce some of their own laws and taxes.
- There were no police, but watchmen kept a lookout for criminals. If one was seen, a great shout went up (called the 'hue and cry') and anyone who heard it was obliged to chase after the criminal.
- The town governments had to deal with all the waste and rubbish produced every day. A channel was set into the middle of the road for foul water to drain away.
- Fire could be a real hazard in towns. Businesses that needed open fires were often sited away from the centre of town to reduce the risk.

★ Make sure you know

- ★ The causes and events of the Peasants' Revolt of 1381.
- ★ The reasons for the downfall of Richard II.
- ★ The typical businesses and people found in a medieval town.
- ★ The position of guilds in medieval towns.
- ★ The issues relating to town government and law and order.

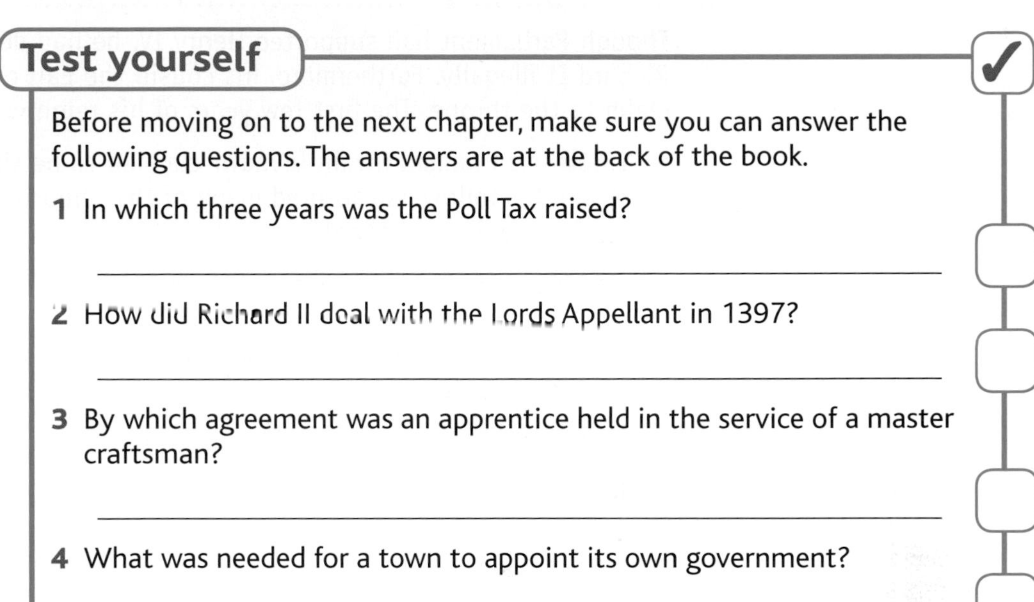

Test yourself

Before moving on to the next chapter, make sure you can answer the following questions. The answers are at the back of the book.

1. In which three years was the Poll Tax raised?
2. How did Richard II deal with the Lords Appellant in 1397?
3. By which agreement was an apprentice held in the service of a master craftsman?
4. What was needed for a town to appoint its own government?

9 The three Henrys

9.1 Henry IV (1399–1413)

Though Parliament had supported Henry IV, he had deposed his cousin Richard II illegally. Furthermore, his cousin the Earl of March had a better claim to the throne. The first few years of his reign were full of troubles.

- A Welshman named Owain Glyndwr claimed to be the true Prince of Wales. He and his followers captured many of the important castles in Wales that had been built by Edward I.
- There was an attempt to replace Henry with the Earl of March in 1403. The rebels joined with Glyndwr and met the King and his son Henry, Prince of Wales, at Shrewsbury on 21 July 1403. In the ensuing battle the rebels were soundly defeated.
- The Scots attempted a rebellion but were swiftly crushed. The French tried to reclaim the English lands in Calais and Gascony, but these attempts also failed.

Henry IV was also notable for his reasonably good relations with Parliament.

- The constant threats to his rule led to expensive military campaigns and Henry faced money problems throughout his reign. However, he was willing to co-operate with Parliament, whose members were mostly supportive of him.
- Parliament appointed royal councillors to help with the King's finances. When Henry's health started to fail him, these men, together with his son Henry, took on more of the King's responsibilities.

Revision tip

You could use index cards to help you remember the main events of Henry IV's reign. Think up suitable questions for the front of the card, with your answers on the back. Then add other cards for Henry V and Henry VI.

9.2 Henry V (1413–22)

Henry V came to the throne with a great deal of military experience. He also kept a tight hold on his finances and strongly supported the Church. But Henry is best known for his campaigns to claim land in France.

- Henry was helped by the fact that France was in the middle of a civil war. The Burgundians and the Armagnacs were fighting each other to gain the throne, and both tried to entice Henry on to their side.
- In August 1415, Henry and his army landed in Normandy. His tactic was to progress deep into France with a *chevauchée* (a fast hit-and-run raid).

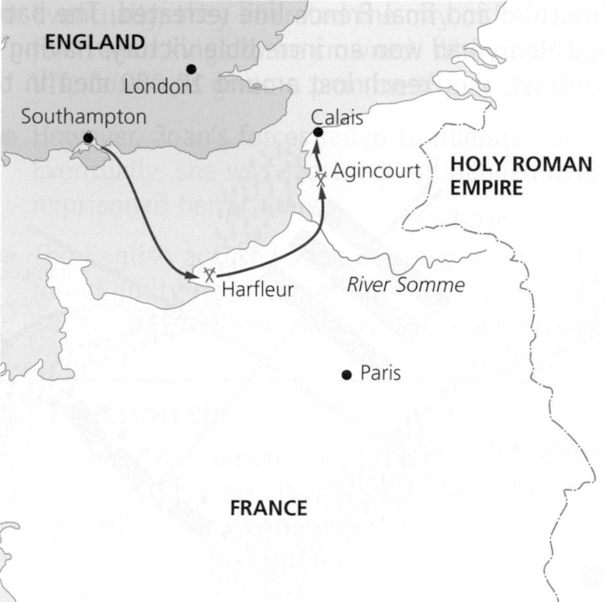

■ Henry V's French campaign of 1415

- The defences at Harfleur were strong and the town did not fall until September. Meanwhile, dysentery had spread through the English ranks and the *chevauchée* had to be abandoned.
- Instead, the English marched north-east along the coast towards Calais. The Armagnacs and Burgundians joined forces to intercept them.
- On 24 October, the English found their path blocked from the north. Some sources wrote that there were as many as 60,000 French soldiers against a force of only 6,000 Englishmen. The two sides took up their positions and waited overnight, just outside the town of Agincourt.

9.3 The Battle of Agincourt, 25 October 1415

- The English lined up in three ranks, with Lord Camoys commanding the group on the left, Henry in the centre and the Duke of York on the right.
- The battlefield lay in a plain with woods on either side, forcing the two armies into a narrow field of combat. The French arranged themselves in three ranks, one behind the other, and simply waited for reinforcements to arrive.
- Henry gave the order for the English to close in on the enemy. The archers planted stakes in the ground to protect them from the French cavalry. The two sides were now only 300 yards apart.
- As the first line of French foot soldiers advanced, the English archers were forced to drop their bows and fight hand to hand. The muddy field hindered the French infantry with their heavy plate armour, and once on the ground it was difficult for them to get up again.
- The second line of French soldiers now had to clamber over piles of bodies to reach the English and the French line gradually fell apart.
- Any French knights still alive were captured and taken to the rear of the English line, to be held for ransom. When a rumour spread that the English were under attack from behind, Henry rashly ordered all the prisoners to be killed.

9.5 Henry VI (1422–71)

Henry VI was finally able to rule his kingdom in 1437. He appeared intelligent and handsome, but was not a natural soldier and did not seem interested in warfare.

- Henry negotiated a truce with France and married Margaret of Anjou, a French noblewoman. Seeing Henry as a weak king, the French seized most of the land that had been lost to the English.
- This was partly the reason for a rebellion in Kent in 1450, led by Jack Cade. The rebels confronted the King in July, demanding that his government be reformed and his councillors replaced.
- After three days, the people of London forced the rebels back over London Bridge and drove them out of the city. Cade was wounded and died before he could face trial.

At this point, Henry's heir was Richard, Duke of York. But Richard had powerful enemies at court who were determined not to let him come to power.

- Queen Margaret had been accused of plotting with the Duke of Suffolk to prevent Henry dealing with Parliament and the Duke of York. After Suffolk's murder, the Duke of Somerset, rather than York, became Henry's closest advisor.
- The situation in France slowly began to improve, with some towns returned to English control. Parliament worked well with the King and agreed to raise taxes.
- But in the summer of 1453, the King suffered a mental collapse and was unable to carry out his duties.

9.6 The coming of civil war

- Richard, Duke of York, became Protector. The Duke of Somerset was arrested and placed in the Tower of London.
- In 1455, the King appeared to recover. York was dismissed and Somerset was freed, becoming Henry's advisor once more. York's supporters feared that they would be arrested.
- York's supporters are termed 'Yorkists' because they supported the Duke of York descended from Edmund of York, the son of Edward III. King Henry's supporters are termed 'Lancastrians' because Henry was descended from John of Gaunt, the Duke of Lancaster, also a son of Edward III (see the family tree on page 190).
- The Yorkists, led by Richard, gathered an army and marched south. On 22 May 1455, they met a Lancastrian army, led by Henry and the Duke of Somerset, at St Albans.
- In the ensuing battle, the Duke of Somerset was killed. Henry VI was captured and forced to restore the Duke of York to his old position of Protector.

★ Make sure you know

- ★ The notable events in the reign of Henry IV.
- ★ The events of Henry V's 1415 French campaign.
- ★ The events of the Battle of Agincourt and its consequences for England and France.
- ★ The life and deeds of Joan of Arc, and her demise.
- ★ The early events of Henry VI's reign.
- ★ The power struggles that led to civil war (the Wars of the Roses).

Test yourself

Before moving on to the next chapter, make sure you can answer the following questions. The answers are at the back of the book.

1 Which Welsh rebel fought at the Battle of Shrewsbury in 1403?

____

2 What was the name for a swift hit-and-run attack, used by Henry V in France?

____

3 What was the charge against Joan of Arc that allowed the English to execute her?

____

4 Who led the Kentish rebellion of 1450?

____

10 The Wars of the Roses

10.1 The first war (1459–61)

■ The Wars of the Roses

The Wars of the Roses are named after the emblems used by the Yorkists and Lancastrians. Richard of York's emblem was the white rose, while the Lancastrians used the red rose.

- In 1459, Queen Margaret declared Richard of York and his supporters to be traitors. Effectively, she was calling for them to be executed.
- The Yorkists seized London and captured Henry VI. Henry and Richard agreed to sign the Act of Accord on 25 October 1460. This declared that Richard would become King on Henry's death.
- An unhappy Margaret gathered a force of Lancastrians in the north. They met the Yorkists at the Battle of Wakefield on 30 December 1460 and Richard of York was killed.
- The Lancastrians defeated another Yorkist force led by Richard Neville, the Earl of Warwick, at St Albans on 22 February 1461, and Henry VI was freed.
- But then the Lancastrians were refused entry into London. Richard of York's son Edward was marching from the West Country with more Yorkists. Fearing this large force, the Lancastrians withdrew, and the Yorkists were allowed into the city.
- The new head of the Yorkists was crowned King Edward IV by his followers. He then led his army in pursuit of the Lancastrians. The two sides met at Towton, in Yorkshire, on 29 March 1461.
- The resulting battle was the largest and bloodiest ever fought in Britain. It is believed that more than 8,000 Lancastrians and 5,000 Yorkists died on that day. Henry VI, Queen Margaret and Prince Edward fled to Scotland. The Yorkist Edward IV was now King of England.

■ **1459** Margaret, wife of Henry VI, declares Richard, Duke of York a traitor.

■ Richard of York and his followers seize London and capture Henry VI.

■ **25 Oct 1460** Act of Accord: Henry to remain as King. Richard of York to be King after him.

■ **30 Dec 1460** Battle of Wakefield: Margaret defeats and kills Richard of York.

■ **22 Feb 1461** Battle of St Albans: Margaret defeats Richard Neville, Earl of Warwick and recaptures Henry VI.

■ Margaret marches to London but is refused entry.

■ Edward, son of Richard of York claims the throne and joins with Richard Neville of Warwick.

■ **29 Mar 1461** Battle of Towton: Edward, son of Richard of York and Richard Neville of Warwick defeat Margaret.

10.2 Edward IV (1461–83)

Edward IV had put the Lancastrian army to flight but his opponents still had many important nobles on their side. The new King therefore could only depend on a few important Yorkist figures. One of these was Richard Neville, the Earl of Warwick.

- Warwick is often known as the 'Kingmaker', because his support was important for a successful claim to the throne.
- However, Warwick soon fell out with Edward. He was annoyed when the King married Elizabeth Woodville, from a rival family who Warwick felt were gaining too much influence.
- Warwick plotted with Edward's brother George, Duke of Clarence, to remove the King from the throne. In 1469, the pair invaded from Calais, but they did not receive support from other nobles and fled back to France.
- Warwick decided to ally with the Lancastrians. Joined by Henry VI and Queen Margaret, he invaded England again in 1470. This time Edward fled the country and Henry VI was back on the throne.

10.3 The second war (1470–71)

- While abroad, Edward was reconciled with his brother George, Duke of Clarence. The brothers raised an army and invaded. At Barnet, north of London, on 14 April 1471, the Lancastrians were defeated and Warwick was killed.
- The Yorkist army met the Lancastrians at the Battle of Tewkesbury on 4 May 1471 and Henry VI's son Prince Edward was killed. Henry was placed in the Tower of London, where he died on 21 May 1471.
- Edward IV's position as King was finally secure. He was generous to his nobles and his own brother Richard, Duke of Gloucester, became extremely powerful and had a lot of influence at court.
- Edward IV died on 9 April 1483, expecting his twelve-year-old son to be crowned Edward V.

■ Edward, son of Richard of York, is now King Edward IV supported by Richard Neville of Warwick, known as 'The Kingmaker'.

■ **1464** Edward IV secretly marries Elizabeth Woodville.

■ **1469** Warwick 'The Kingmaker' joins Edward IV's brother George, Duke of Clarence, and invades England.

■ **1470** Edward IV drives Warwick out of the country.

■ Warwick joins up with Queen Margaret and Henry VI, and invades again.

■ Edward IV is forced to flee the country.

■ **1471** Edward IV joins with his brother George of Clarence.

■ **14 Apr 1471** Battle of Barnet: Edward IV and George of Clarence defeat and kill Warwick.

■ **4 May 1471** Battle of Tewkesbury: Edward IV defeats Queen Margaret and kills Prince Edward.

■ **21 May 1471** Mad old King Henry VI dies in the Tower of London. Edward IV is safely King again.

■ Edward's brother Richard, Duke of Gloucester, becomes very powerful.

■ **1478** Edward's other brother George of Clarence is executed for treason, drowned, according to some, in a barrel of wine.

■ **9 April 1483** Edward IV dies leaving a twelve-year-old son, Edward V, as King.

10.4 Edward V and Richard III (1483–85)

On his father's death, the young King Edward V found himself in the middle of a power struggle. His mother's family, the Woodvilles, battled with his father's brother Richard, Duke of Gloucester, to control him.

- Richard used his position to have his opponents executed. King Edward and his younger brother Prince Richard were placed in the Tower of London, supposedly for their own safekeeping.
- In July 1483, Richard declared that the marriage of Edward IV and Elizabeth Woodville had been invalid. Therefore the two brothers were illegitimate and Edward was not the rightful King.
- Instead, Richard argued, as the next in line to the throne, *he* should be crowned King Richard III. This was done on 6 July 1483 and the two 'Princes in the Tower' were never seen again.
- Nobody is quite sure what happened to the two boys, but most historians agree that they were murdered in the Tower, and probably by men working on the orders of Richard III.

Richard III had a short and unsettled reign. He was popular among the northern nobles, but viewed with suspicion in the south. By the end of 1483, there were rumours circulating about the fate of the Princes in the Tower and the King's involvement.

- In November 1483, there was a revolt against Richard by an important ally, the Duke of Buckingham, which the King managed to put down. The following year Richard's son and wife both died, leaving him without an heir.
- The main threat to his rule came from the Earl of Richmond, Henry Tudor, who had a weak claim to the throne. Henry had supported Buckingham in the 1483 revolt but had escaped to France.
- With French support, Henry sailed to Wales in August 1485 and gathered an army. They met Richard's forces on 22 August, outside the town of Market Bosworth in Leicestershire.

10.5 The Battle of Bosworth, 22 August 1485

- The armies took up their positions: Richard's on the top of Ambion Hill; Henry's near the marshes below. For the Yorkists, the Duke of Norfolk commanded the front rank and the Earl of Northumberland the rear. Henry's smaller army was led by the Earl of Oxford.
- Lord Thomas Stanley and Sir William Stanley had been supporters of the King. Richard hoped that they would stay loyal and fight for him. At Bosworth, the Stanleys' armies stood to one side to see what would happen.
- Norfolk led his forces down the hill to meet Oxford's ranks. In the vicious hand-to-hand fighting, Norfolk was killed.

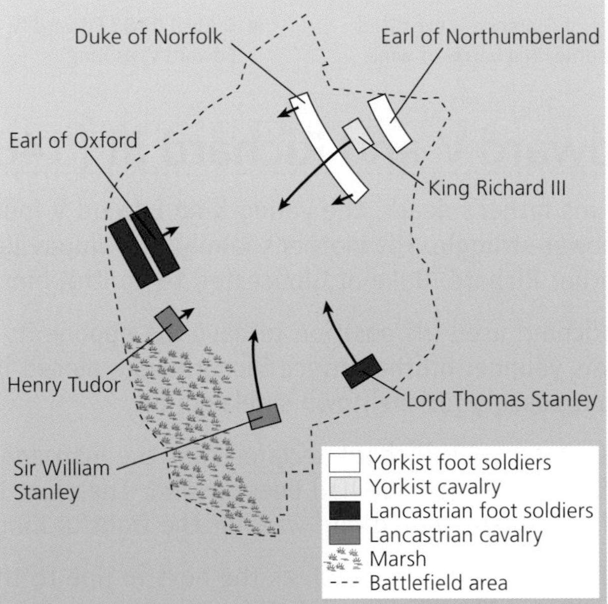

■ The Battle of Bosworth

- Henry rode towards the Stanleys, appealing for them to join him. Seeing Henry now unprotected, Richard led his close guard in a cavalry charge across the battlefield.
- The Stanleys saw the threat to Henry and at this moment decided to join his side. They intercepted Richard before he could reach his target.
- Meanwhile, Richard's rear division, led by the Earl of Northumberland, watched the King's downfall from the top of Ambion Hill. It seems that they too had decided to support Henry.
- Richard's horse was killed underneath him and he was cut down trying to fight back on foot.
- At the death of Richard III, the Yorkist armies rode off. Richard's crown was retrieved by Lord Stanley and placed on the head of Henry Tudor, who was now declared King Henry VII.

? **Evidence question**

You may be asked to answer an evidence question on Richard III. Refer to the guidance on page xi and make sure that you practise answering these questions.

★ Make sure you know

- ★ The causes and events of the First War of the Roses (1459–61).
- ★ The notable events of the reign of Edward VI.
- ★ The causes and events of the Second War of the Roses (1470–71).
- ★ The possible fate of Edward V and his brother Richard (the 'Princes in the Tower').
- ★ The threats to the reign of Richard III.
- ★ The events and outcome of the Battle of Bosworth.

Test yourself

Before moving on to the next chapter, make sure you can answer the following questions. The answers are at the back of the book.

1 What were the two symbols of the Yorkists and the Lancastrians?

____

2 By which nickname is Richard Neville, Earl of Warwick, often known?

____

3 At which battle was Henry VI's son Edward killed?

____

4 On what grounds did Richard III claim that Edward V was not the rightful King?

____

5 Which Yorkist commander failed to come to the aid of Richard III at the Battle of Bosworth?

____

PART B
THE MAKING OF THE UNITED KINGDOM
1485–1750

Henry VII (1485–1509)

11.1 Securing the throne

Henry was unprepared to become King. He had no experience of government and had been in exile for many years. He used several methods to hold on to his throne.

Uniting the country

- Henry knew that a country divided by war was not stable. He therefore took steps to unite the two sides.
- Henry married his cousin Elizabeth of York, the daughter of Edward IV and sister of Edward V. This was done both to unite the houses of Lancaster and York, and to satisfy anyone who felt that the throne should have passed to Elizabeth on the death of her uncle, Richard III.

Controlling the nobility

- Henry needed a nobility that was strong enough to support him, but not strong enough to turn against him. Many nobles had been killed in the Wars of the Roses. Henry replaced them with educated men from lower classes who served him in government.
- Yorkists were stripped of their titles and had their lands confiscated. Lancastrians who had been deprived of their lands by Edward IV had them restored.
- The Court of Star Chamber dealt with any rebellion among the nobility. Punishments included fines and the further confiscation of land from traitors.
- Justices of the Peace were appointed to help maintain law and order, and keep the court system working.

Retaining

- Retaining was the practice of holding a personal army. Henry believed it was potentially dangerous for nobles to keep private armies, which might instead be used against him.
- The Law of Livery restricted the number of soldiers that lords were allowed to keep. They also had to sign a recognisance, whereby they agreed to forfeit a large sum of money if they acted disloyally.

The Council

- Henry began to take away the nobles' right to attend his Council, which started to become full of educated men who were serving the King's government, such as Richard Empson, Edmund Dudley, Edward Poynings and Reginald Bray.
- Men like these were appointed to run the Court of Star Chamber and the Court of Requests. There was also a court set up to control retaining.

- Henry also set up the Council of Wales and re-started the Council of the North. This was to extend his power into areas where he had not had much support from the nobles.

Revision tip

Try using index cards to help you remember how Henry VII secured his throne. The first card could have questions or a numbered list for the four points: uniting, controlling, retaining and council. Then have four further cards covering the detail of each of the points.

Essay question

Try this sample essay question for yourself. A suggested answer is given at the back of the book.

Q Explain how Henry VII dealt with opposition to his rule. (30)

11.2 The two pretenders

Henry's treatment of the nobles meant that he was unpopular with many of them. Because of this, the King faced several serious uprisings that threatened to remove him from the throne.

Lambert Simnel

- Edward, the Earl of Warwick, was a strong claimant to the throne, so Henry locked him up in the Tower of London.
- In 1486, Richard Symonds, an Oxford priest, began to claim that one of his pupils, named Lambert Simnel, was actually the Earl of Warwick.
- Simnel was taken to Ireland and crowned King Edward VI by his supporters. They gathered an army of Yorkists and sailed to England.
- At the Battle of East Stoke on 16 June 1487 the rebels were heavily defeated. Simnel himself was pardoned and given a job in the royal kitchens.

Perkin Warbeck

- Perkin Warbeck claimed to be Richard of York, the younger of the two 'Princes in the Tower'. He went to Ireland in 1491 and was acclaimed as the true King of England.
- In 1492–93, he travelled around Europe gaining support and was proclaimed King Richard IV. In 1495, he went to Scotland, gained the backing of King James IV and married one of his relatives.
- Henry VII's spies reported that his old friend William Stanley was one of Warbeck's supporters and he was put to death.
- In 1497, Warbeck joined the rebellion in Cornwall (see page 58) but he was arrested and taken to London.
- When Warbeck tried to escape, he was placed in the Tower of London with the Earl of Warwick. When the two were suspected of plotting another escape, they were both put to death in November 1499.

Revision tip

You could use a flow chart to help you remember what happened to the two pretenders. The diagram below shows what part of the chart might look like.

The two pretenders

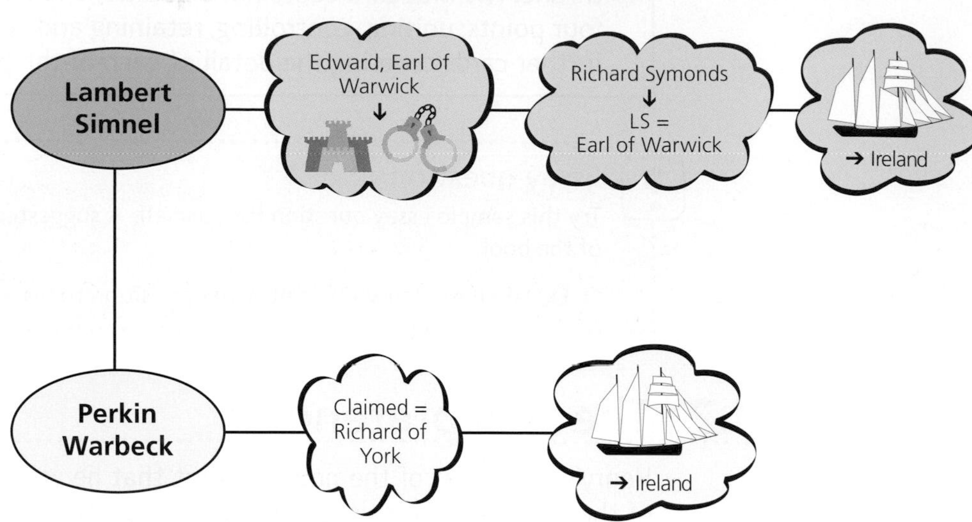

11.3 The tax rebellions

- Traditionally, people in the southern counties of England paid taxes to fund wars against France, and those in the northern counties paid to fund wars against Scotland.
- In 1489, Henry tried to gain funding for a war against France in the north as well as the south. The people of Yorkshire rebelled and killed the Earl of Northumberland.
- Henry's army managed to put down the uprising fairly easily and the rebel leaders were hanged at York.
- In 1497, the Cornish decided to rebel against taxation and gained the support of a noble, Lord Audley. They were also joined by the pretender Perkin Warbeck (see page 57).
- The Cornish rebels gathered a force and marched to London. But they were easily defeated by the King's army and the leaders were executed.

Revision tip

Set out the main points about the tax rebellions on a chart. Use a different branch for each of the bullet points above. Remember to use pictures and different colours.

11.4 Foreign policy

- Henry's dealings with other countries reflected his desire for a secure throne. He knew that the pretenders Simnel and Warbeck had been encouraged by foreign powers.
- In 1489, Henry signed the Treaty of Medina del Campo with Spain. It was agreed that his son Arthur would marry Catherine of Aragon, the daughter of King Ferdinand of Spain. The marriage took place in 1501, but Prince Arthur died the following year.
- In 1492, Henry signed the Treaty of Etaples with France. Charles VIII of France had pledged his support for Perkin Warbeck. The English invaded France and demanded that the pretender be handed over.
- In 1502, Henry signed the Treaty of Perpetual Peace with Scotland. Henry and James IV of Scotland agreed to stop fighting each other and it was decided that James would marry Henry's daughter Margaret.

★ Make sure you know

★ The methods Henry VII used to secure his place on the throne.

★ The events and consequences of the rebellions of Lambert Simnel and Perkin Warbeck.

★ The events of the tax rebellions faced by Henry VII.

★ The key points behind Henry VII's foreign policy.

Test yourself

Before moving on to the next chapter, make sure you can answer the following questions. The answers are at the back of the book.

1 What was the practice of holding a personal army called?

____

2 Who did Perkin Warbeck claim to be?

____

3 Which noble joined the Cornish tax rebels in 1497?

____

4 By which treaty was the marriage between Prince Arthur and Catherine of Aragon arranged?

____

Henry VIII (1509–47)

12.1 Early life and reign

Henry VII's elder son Arthur had died in 1502, so when the King himself died in 1509, the throne passed to his younger son, who became Henry VIII.

- Henry was not expected to become King and his father intended him to have a career in the Church. The young prince therefore became devoted to religion.
- Henry could speak Latin, French, Italian and Spanish. He loved music, composing many pieces himself, and also wrote poetry. He was also enthusiastic about works of art and architecture.
- Henry was athletic and extremely good at sports. He was strong and much taller than most men of the time.
- This age is often known as the Renaissance, which means 're-birth'. People rediscovered the beauty of classical culture from ancient Rome and Greece, and this influenced education and the arts in particular. Henry is sometimes called a Renaissance prince.

Revision tip

Draw a sketch to help you remember what happened in the early part of Henry VIII's reign and the sort of man he was. Include all the different elements of his character – the things he loved doing and what he was good at, and so on.

12.2 Thomas Wolsey

Thomas Wolsey was a royal official who rose to become Henry VIII's chief minister in the early part of his reign. He became Lord Chancellor and then Archbishop of York, and was sometimes given the title *alter rex*, meaning the 'other king'.

Wolsey and finance

Henry VIII's lavish court cost money that Wolsey had to raise.

- Wolsey introduced a tax called the subsidy, which determined how much tax an individual had to pay by assessing their wealth.
- Wolsey carried on squeezing the rich nobles in the same way that Henry VII had done. They were forced to give gifts of money, known as benevolences, to the King. In return their estates and positions were secured.
- Wolsey went too far when he tried to raise money for expensive wars. In 1525, the King needed funds for a planned invasion of France, and Wolsey tried raising a tax called the Amicable Grant. There was so much opposition that it had to be abandoned.

Wolsey and law

- Wolsey re-established the Court of Star Chamber and the Court of Chancery. The Court of Requests was also re-introduced to hear cases free of charge for the poor.
- Wolsey carried out enquiries into the process of enclosure (see page 82). Because of enclosure, the lower classes were left without jobs or land. Wolsey, while supporting the process, was concerned that many landholders were doing it illegally. There were enquiries held about the issue in 1517, 1518 and 1526.

Wolsey and the Church

- In 1518, Wolsey was appointed to be the Pope's legate in England. He became determined to correct any abuses in the English Church.
- Nonetheless, he was guilty of several abuses himself. Wolsey held more than one position, which was called pluralism. Wolsey also sold church positions for money – the abuse of simony – and did not visit the areas under his control as regularly as he should have.
- In these ways, Wolsey enjoyed a lavish lifestyle. He displayed his wealth by building Hampton Court Palace.

Wolsey and foreign policy

- Wolsey's aim was to make England as important and powerful as the three main powers in Europe at that time: France, Spain and the Holy Roman Empire.
- In 1518, the leaders of all three met with Wolsey and Henry VIII in London. A peace treaty was signed and it was agreed that Henry's daughter Mary would marry Louis, the son of Francis I of France.
- Maximilian I, the Holy Roman Emperor, died in 1519 and Charles I of Spain was elected to rule his Empire as well as Spain. Henry and Francis had both hoped to become Holy Roman Emperor and now they felt threatened by Charles.
- The two kings met near Calais in June 1520. The meeting was organised by Wolsey and was an opportunity for Henry to show off his wealth and power. It became known as the 'Field of the Cloth of Gold' and was supposed to be a display of friendship, but the two kings remained wary of each other.

Revision tip

Why not map out the key points in a chart to show the influence Thomas Wolsey had. Write the word 'Thomas' in the centre of the page and then draw four branches, marked 'finance', 'law', 'church' and 'foreign policy'. Use pictures to sum up the key points and different colours for the different branches.

12.3 The rise of Protestantism

- The Church played an important role in everybody's life during the sixteenth century. But some people started to question the way it was run.
- A common practice was the selling of indulgences and the charging of money to visitors who wanted to pray over the relics of certain saints.
- The Church had gained great wealth through these practices. People began to resent the fact that this money was spent on supporting the lifestyles of churchmen, rather than being given to the poor and needy.
- Church services were conducted in Latin, which generally only priests could read. Some people started to argue that the Bible should be translated into English for ordinary people to read themselves.
- In 1517, a German monk named Martin Luther nailed a list of 95 points for reform to the door of a church in Wittenberg.
- Luther's ideas became a movement known as Protestantism. Protestants criticised practices such as the selling of indulgences and the worship of relics, and argued for translations of the Bible.
- A key argument was over the issue of bread and wine in church services. Catholics believed that the bread and wine were actually transformed into the body and blood of Christ (a process known as transubstantiation). Protestants argued that the bread and wine were only supposed to represent and commemorate the body and blood.
- Henry VIII began as a strong supporter of Catholic views. He wrote a book attacking Luther and was rewarded by the Pope with the title *Fidei Defensor*, which means 'Defender of the Faith'.

Revision tip

You could plot out the rise of Protestantism in the form of a chart, with different branches for each of the different elements – 'problems with the Church', 'Martin Luther', 'bread and wine', 'Henry's views'.

12.4 The King's Great Matter

In 1509, Henry VIII married Catherine of Aragon, the widow of his brother, Arthur.

- Henry wanted a strong male heir to continue the Tudor line, but the only surviving child from his marriage to Catherine of Aragon was a girl, Mary, born in 1516.
- Henry believed that he was being punished by God for marrying his brother's widow. He convinced himself that his marriage was invalid and Wolsey was instructed to seek an annulment from the Pope.
- In 1529, the Pope sent Cardinal Campeggio to England to preside over a court to debate the issue. The court failed to reach a decision.
- Henry blamed Wolsey for his failure to secure the annulment. He was charged with treason, but died in 1530 before he could be brought to trial.

- Henry appointed Thomas Cranmer to be Archbishop of Canterbury. Cranmer held many Protestant views and was known to support an annulment. He secretly married Henry and Anne Boleyn in January 1533 and annulled the marriage to Catherine.
- The Pope excommunicated Henry. But Henry now believed that he, and not the Pope, should be in charge of the Church in England.
- In September 1533, Anne gave birth to Henry's child. To the King's huge disappointment, it was another girl – Elizabeth.

12.5 Cromwell and the Reformation

Thomas Cromwell was Henry's chief advisor and, like Cranmer, was sympathetic to the Protestant cause. In what has since become known as the Reformation Parliament, Cromwell used his influence to pass several laws.

The Reformation Parliament

- The Act in Restraint of Annates (1532) stopped the English Church making payments to the Pope.
- The Statute in Restraint of Appeals (1533) declared that England was ruled by a king who had 'whole and entire authority' within it. Therefore any excommunications from Rome of English people were invalid and the English were forbidden from appealing to the Pope.
- The Act of Succession (1533) declared that the marriage of Henry VIII and Catherine of Aragon had been invalid and that Princess Mary was therefore illegitimate. The Act stated that the throne would pass to the children of Henry and Anne Boleyn instead.
- The Act of Supremacy (1534) declared that Henry was the head of the English Church, not the Pope.
- The Treason Act (1534) stated that anyone who argued against Henry's position as head of the English Church would face a charge of treason. Two victims of this law were John Fisher, the Bishop of Rochester, and Sir Thomas More, Henry's former Lord Chancellor. Both men were executed in 1535.
- The First Fruits and Tenths Act (1534) allowed Henry to take the first year's earnings from all bishoprics and church offices. Thereafter he would take one-tenth of any further earnings.

Revision tip

Think up a silly story, using the first letters of each of the Acts, to help you remember the order they were passed:

Act of **R**estraint of **An**nates (1532)	RANdy
Statute in **R**estraint of **Ap**peals (1533)	RAPper
Act of **Suc**cession (1533)	SUCked down his
Act of **Sup**remacy (1534)	SoUP with
Treason Act (1534)	TREAcle,
First **Fruit**s and **Te**nths Act (1534)	FRUIT and TEa

See *Study Skills*, page 66 for help with this.

Dissolution of the Monasteries

The 'break with Rome' provoked the Catholic countries of Spain and France to declare war on England, which was encouraged by the Pope. Henry now needed money to defend England.

- In the 1520s, Cromwell had helped Thomas Wolsey to close down the most corrupt monasteries. He now believed that the process could be continued and all the wealth of these houses given over to the Crown.
- In 1536, Parliament passed the First Act of Dissolution that allowed the smaller monasteries to be closed down. This was followed in 1539 by the Second Act of Dissolution, which dealt with the larger monasteries.
- Local landowners were very pleased to buy the land and buildings of the monastery for their own uses.

The Pilgrimage of Grace

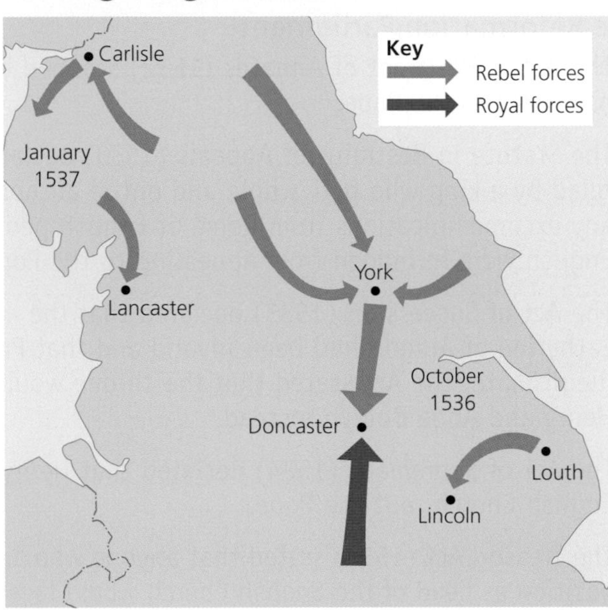

The opposition to the Dissolution of the Monasteries came from local people who took up arms against Cromwell's men.

- At Lincoln in 1536, a force of 10,000 men attacked the commissioners and occupied the cathedral.
- In Yorkshire, a lawyer named Robert Aske and a noble named Lord Darcy gathered 30,000 men together. The movement became known as the Pilgrimage of Grace.
- Aske drew up a petition in December 1536, calling for an end to heresy and declaring that Princess Mary was legitimate.
- Aske marched south with his men, claiming to be leading a pilgrimage, not a rebellion. He declared that they did not intend to attack the King but to free him from the influences of advisors like Cromwell.
- The Duke of Norfolk met the rebels at Doncaster and promised to hold a Parliament to discuss their complaints. But Henry had no intention of keeping these promises and the ringleaders were executed.

? Evidence question

You may be asked to answer an evidence question on Henry VIII and the Reformation. Refer to the guidance on page xi and make sure that you practise answering these questions.

The Ten Articles (1536) and the Six Articles (1539)

Cromwell wanted to make the English Church more Protestant and urged Parliament to pass the Act of Ten Articles in 1536.

- The Church now only recognised three sacraments: baptism, penance and the Eucharist. The Bible was translated into English and priests were allowed to marry.
- The other Catholic sacraments of confirmation, ordination, marriage and the last rites were now no longer regarded as holy sacraments. Pilgrimages and the display of relics were also banned.

But despite his treatment of the Church, Henry still regarded himself as Catholic. Cromwell was in danger of making England a wholly Protestant country, which the King did not want. So in 1539, the Ten Articles were modified by the Six Articles, which reintroduced many Catholic beliefs.

- The idea of transubstantiation was confirmed. The people could now take only bread at the Communion, not wine, and were encouraged to confess their sins to a priest. Priests were once again banned from marrying.
- Henry produced the King's Book, which prohibited many kinds of people from reading the new English Bible.

12.6 The six wives of Henry VIII

Revision tip

The fates of Henry VIII's six wives can be remembered by means of a well-known ditty:

Divorced, beheaded, died;
divorced, beheaded, survived.

Catherine of Aragon

- Catherine was Henry's first wife. Henry had their marriage annulled when it became obvious she was not going to produce a son.

Anne Boleyn

- Anne had given Henry a daughter, Elizabeth, but she was the only one of their children who survived. Henry became convinced that he was being punished. He had also fallen in love with another courtier, Jane Seymour, and wanted to be rid of his wife.
- Cromwell accused Anne of treason, adultery and incest – charges that are now believed to be untrue. She was tried, found guilty and executed in May 1536.

Jane Seymour

- Henry then married Jane Seymour and in October 1536 she gave birth to a boy, whom the delighted King named Edward.
- However, soon after the birth, Jane developed puerperal fever and died twelve days later.

Anne of Cleves

- It was suggested that Henry marry Anne of Cleves for political reasons. Henry decided to marry her based on her portrait by Hans Holbein.
- A few days before the wedding, Henry met Anne and was not impressed. By this time, it was impossible to back out and the ceremony went ahead. Henry and Anne agreed to annul the marriage six months later.

Catherine Howard

- Henry was angry with Cromwell for the part he had played in the marriage to Anne of Cleves. He was accused of heresy and executed in July 1540.
- Henry married Catherine Howard in the same month. However, Catherine committed adultery against the King. She was tried for treason, found guilty and executed in February 1542.

Catherine Parr

- Henry married Catherine Parr in July 1543. She persuaded him to make amends with his two daughters.
- Henry's will, made on 30 December 1546, declared that the throne would pass first to his son Edward, then to any children he might have with Catherine Parr, then to Mary, Elizabeth and the daughters of his sister Mary Rose.

Henry VIII died a month later, on 28 January 1547 and his throne passed to his nine-year-old son, who became Edward VI.

Revision tip

Try using a chart with separate sections to help you remember the details about Henry VIII's wives. Have a different branch/section for each of the wives.

★ Make sure you know

★ The events of Henry VIII's early life and the main points of his personality.

★ The influence of Thomas Wolsey on Henry VIII's government.

★ The key ideas of Protestantism and the events surrounding its rise.

★ The events and consequences of the annulment of Henry VIII's marriage to Catherine of Aragon.

★ The acts of Thomas Cromwell and the events of the English Reformation.

★ The events surrounding the marriages and fates of Henry VIII's six wives.

Test yourself

Before moving on to the next chapter, make sure you can answer the following questions. The answers are at the back of the book.

1 What were benevolences?

2 What was the name of the meeting between Henry VIII and Francis I near Calais in June 1520?

3 Why was Henry VIII awarded the title *Fidei Defensor*?

4 Why did Henry VIII want his marriage to Catherine of Aragon to be annulled?

5 Which Act of Parliament allowed Henry VIII to take a portion of the earnings from church offices?

6 The Act of Ten Articles allowed which three church sacraments to be recognised?

Ireland and rebellion

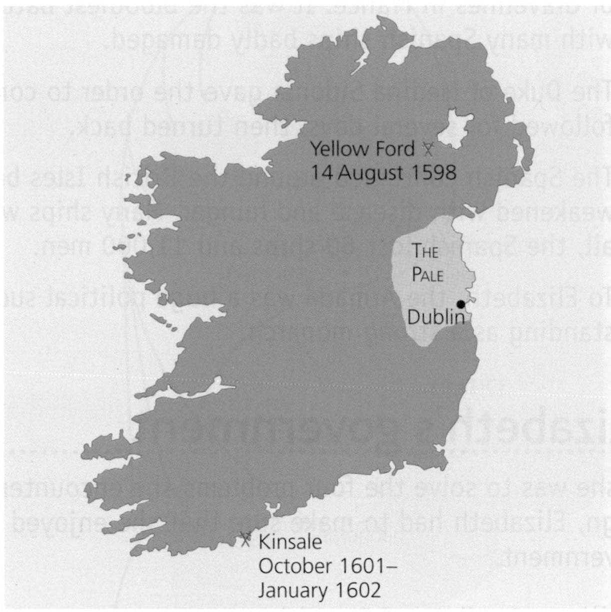

■ The wars in Ireland

- Elizabeth's good relations with her government were vital in dealing with trouble in Ireland. Her officials controlled an area of land around Dublin known as the Pale. The rest of Ireland was controlled by independent nobles.
- Ireland had also remained Catholic and was therefore a potential base from which a foreign Catholic country could launch an invasion of England.
- In 1598, an Irish noble named Hugh O'Neill, the Earl of Tyrone, defeated an English force at the Battle of Yellow Ford. This allowed him to rule over much of Ireland.
- Elizabeth's favourite, the Earl of Essex, was sent to restore English authority to Ireland. But this campaign was a dismal failure and Essex returned to England. He blamed Elizabeth's ministers for turning the Queen against him and, in 1601, gathered a small rebel force to fight in London. This failed, too, and he was executed for treason.
- In the meantime, Lord Mountjoy had more success in Ireland. He defeated the Irish in a series of battles at Kinsale during the winter of 1601–02.

Elizabeth died in 1603, having dealt effectively with most of the problems that she had encountered. Her army and navy had successfully fought off any attempts to invade. The Elizabethan Settlement had proved to be an inclusive way of bringing about religious harmony, at least for the time being. And, while foreign wars had been expensive, the economy was much more stable than at the beginning of her reign. But one problem remained: the question of who would succeed her. Elizabeth never married and had no children. On her deathbed, she named as her choice the son of Mary, Queen of Scots, King James VI of Scotland. He came to the English throne as James I of England.

★ Make sure you know

- ★ The four main problems facing Elizabeth I during her reign.
- ★ The terms of the Elizabethan Settlement.
- ★ The events surrounding the imprisonment and execution of Mary, Queen of Scots.
- ★ The events of Elizabeth I's war with Spain.
- ★ The acts of Elizabeth's government.

Test yourself

Before moving on to the next chapter, make sure you can answer the following questions. The answers are at the back of the book.

1 How did the Act of Supremacy (1559) make a small concession to Catholics?

2 Who was the head of Elizabeth I's secret service?

3 Which battle was the bloodiest of the Spanish Armada campaign of 1588?

4 Which noble led the Irish uprising against Elizabeth I during the years 1598–1602?

Life in the sixteenth century

15.1 Trade

In the sixteenth century, England began to change from a country in which the wealth came from the land (agriculture), to one in which the wealth came from the sale of manufactured goods (trade).

- By the Elizabethan period, England was trading successfully with other countries in Europe. English cloth was popular in France and the Netherlands. Other materials, such as iron, salt, sugar, coal and wool, were sent all over Europe.
- English ports became more important. Towns such as Bristol and Liverpool became industrialised, and grew quickly.
- Merchants gained their wealth by buying the materials from locals in England, manufacturing the goods and selling them to foreign buyers at a higher price.
- As adventurers including Sir Francis Drake explored faraway countries such as the Americas, new trade routes opened up and produced more opportunities for merchants.
- These expeditions were risky and merchants began to join together and form joint stock companies.
- The merchants sold shares in these companies to rich landowners and the government promised these companies a monopoly if they opened up trade routes to new countries.
- London's docks grew as more quays were built for loading and unloading. Elizabeth introduced legal quays with the sole right to receive goods from overseas.

Revision tip

Draw a picture to depict the growth in trade during the Elizabethan period or make up a story. Include all the different elements, from the growth of different towns to the explorers such as Sir Francis Drake.

15.2 Poverty and the Poor Laws

The sixteenth century also saw a huge increase in the number of poor people in England. One cause for this was the lack of jobs and there were several reasons for this:

- The enclosure movement (see page 82) and the change from arable to pastoral farming meant that a much smaller workforce was needed.
- The Dissolution of the Monasteries meant that people who had previously been monks and nuns now had to find work.

- The clampdown on retaining meant that soldiers were left without work.
- The population of England rose by more than 1 million in the sixteenth century.

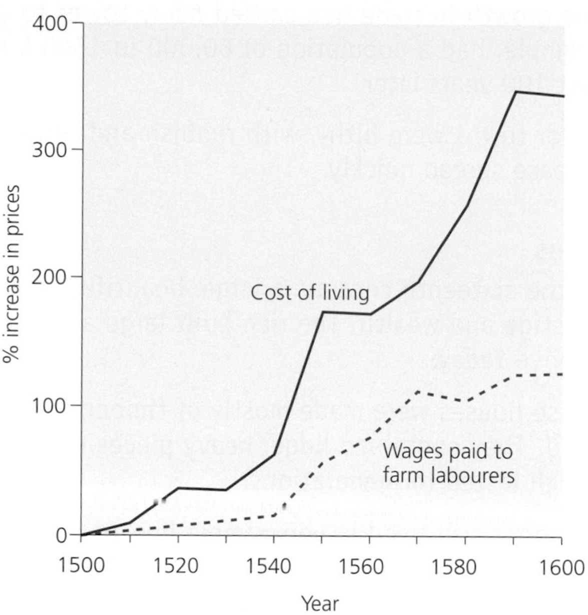

■ The rate of inflation during the sixteenth century

Another cause of poverty was the rise in inflation and there were several reasons for this.

- There was increased demand for everyday foods, but not enough to go around. The price of this food rose as people competed to buy it.
- Governments debased the coinage, reducing the amount of precious metal in each coin.
- Foreign wars were expensive to fund.
- There were a number of bad harvests.

The governments of Henry VIII, Edward VI and Mary I did not take steps to stop people being poor in the first place. They were more concerned with the threat to law and order posed by beggars.

- In 1547, Parliament passed an Act declaring that vagrants could be branded, whipped and sent back to their home parish. Some were imprisoned or even killed.

In 1597 and 1601, the government of Elizabeth I passed a series of Poor Laws. These were enacted to offer help to the poorest people. They defined two classes of poor:

- The deserving poor were those unable to work. A tax called the Poor Rate was collected from the rich by the Overseers of the Poor. This money helped the deserving poor, either through indoor relief in the parish poorhouse or by outdoor relief in their own homes.
- The idle poor – those who did not work because they were lazy – were to be whipped and sent back to their home parish. If they carried on begging they were sent to a House of Correction or even hanged.

15.3 Town and country

Towns

- The growth in trade had caused many towns to grow quickly. London, for example, had a population of 60,000 in 1500 but had grown to 250,000 just 100 years later.
- Tudor towns were filthy, with rubbish and sewage lying in the streets, and disease spread quickly.

Homes

- In the sixteenth century, a large, beautiful home was a sign of the owner's prestige and wealth. The rich built large and ornate houses, some of which survive today.
- These houses were made mostly of timber, with the roof being thatched or tiled. They contained huge, heavy pieces of furniture, usually made of oak, which lasted for generations.
- The poor still lived in very simple houses with only one or two rooms. Furniture was very basic and most people slept on the bare earth floor.

Pastimes

- Music and dancing were very popular in Tudor times. The richer households owned keyboard instruments such as the spinet or virginals. Poorer people sometimes played the lute or flute.
- Sports were also common in towns and villages, especially team sports such as football. Thankfully, sports such as bear-baiting and cock-fighting have been outlawed today.
- The theatre was also popular and this encouraged the writing of famous plays by Marlowe, Johnson and – of course – Shakespeare (see page 102).

Enclosure

- Enclosure was a two-part process: first, the division of open fields; second, the enclosure of the common land.
- In medieval times, England used an open-field system, in which farmers rented a strip of land on a large field. Enclosure meant that the lords withdrew the lease of the land and enclosed the field for grazing animals.
- The lords also fenced off the common land and began to use it for their own livestock.
- The local people resented the changes and this sometimes provoked revolts such as Kett's Rebellion (see page 69).
- Enclosure allowed the wool trade to grow. The government raised more money through the taxes paid on exporting wool to foreign countries.

Revision tip

You could map out what life was like in the towns and countryside of Elizabethan England. Use a different branch for each of the headings above. You should be able to include lots of different pictures instead of words to help you visualise what went on. Try using the one on the next page as a starting point and add in the sub-branches.

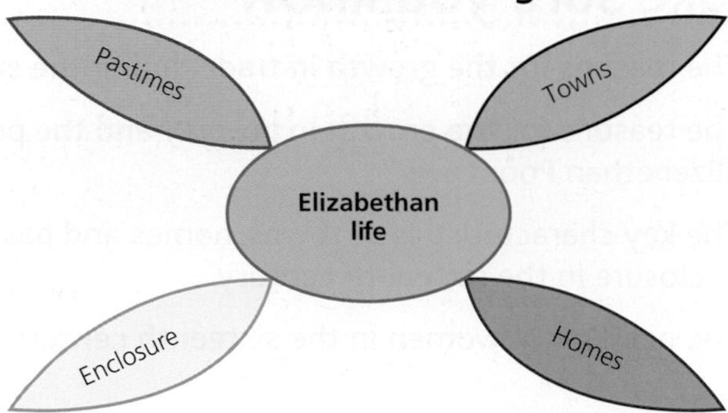

Essay question

Try this sample essay question for yourself. A suggested answer is given at the back of the book.

Q Explain how the process of enclosure led to unrest in the countryside. (30)

15.4 Women in the sixteenth century

The role of women had not changed much since medieval times. Women were still believed to be inferior to men and it was this way of thinking that had made Henry VIII so determined to have a male heir.

- A husband was legally responsible for all his family. He was allowed to sell off any land and property that his wife had owned before their marriage. If she committed adultery, she could be punished severely.
- Girls were generally only taught how to perform household tasks. These tasks would include cooking and food preparation, cleaning, washing and sewing. Only very rich women were taught to read and write.
- Marriages were often carried out to increase the wealth of both families. The bride gave a dowry as a contribution to the household, which might have been a gift of money, land or property.
- Pregnancy was dangerous and the death of the mother during childbirth was not uncommon. Even if a birth was successful, the mother could contract a post-natal illness, such as puerperal fever.
- The wives of rich husbands spent much of their time at leisure, though they did have to make sure that their servants were running the household properly.
- Poorer women had to look after the children and cook meals themselves, and often had to help their husbands working in the fields.
- Women dressed both to suit the Tudor fashions and to show off their wealth. The clothes were sometimes very ornate and heavy.

★ Make sure you know

- ★ The reasons for the growth in trade during the sixteenth century.
- ★ The reasons for the growth in poverty and the provisions of the Elizabethan Poor Laws.
- ★ The key characteristics of towns, homes and pastimes, and the process of enclosure in the sixteenth century.
- ★ The position of women in the sixteenth century.

Test yourself

Before moving on to the next chapter, make sure you can answer the following questions. The answers are at the back of the book.

1 How could companies obtain a monopoly?

2 What was the difference between the deserving poor and the idle poor?

3 How did the process of enclosure provide more money for the government through taxes?

4 What was the main household task for the wives of rich husbands?

16 James I (1603–25) and Charles I (1625–49)

16.1 James I and religion

Unlike his mother, Mary, Queen of Scots, James was brought up as a Protestant. He became James VI of Scotland at the age of one, when his mother was forced to abdicate the Scottish throne and pass power to him. When Elizabeth died, James was proclaimed King James I of England.

- Puritans hoped that James would stamp out Catholicism in England once and for all. The Millenary Petition demanded the removal of bishops and alterations to make the *Book of Common Prayer* more radical.
- But at a Church conference at Hampton Court Palace in 1604, James refused to dismiss the bishops.
- Some Puritans decided to leave England to start a new life elsewhere. One group of these were the Pilgrim Fathers, who sailed to America on the *Mayflower* in September 1620.
- James did agree to a new English translation of the Bible. This work was called the *Authorised Version* and is today often known as the King James Bible.

Revision tip

Use pictures to help you remember the main points with regard to James I and religion. You could draw a series of sketches depicting, for example, James refusing to dismiss the bishops and the Pilgrim Fathers setting sail for America.

The Gunpowder Plot (1605)

- In 1604, two Catholics named Robert Catesby and Thomas Percy devised a plan to assassinate James by blowing up the Houses of Parliament as he opened the session. The date for the attempt was to be 5 November 1605.
- On 26 October 1605, another plotter named Francis Tresham wrote to his brother-in-law Lord Monteagle, warning him not to attend the opening of Parliament for his own safety. Monteagle passed the letter on to the authorities.
- On the night of 4 November, a plotter named Guy Fawkes was arrested in a cellar underneath Parliament. Under torture, he revealed the names of the conspirators and within a few days they had all been arrested or killed in skirmishes. They were hanged, drawn and quartered the following year.
- Some historians suggest that the men were framed by James' government and the false plot was invented as an excuse to pass anti-Catholic laws.

Revision tip

Most people can remember the rhyme about the Gunpowder Plot:

Remember, remember the fifth of November
Gunpowder, treason and plot.
I see no reason why gunpowder, treason
Should ever be forgot.

Try making up a phrase or rhyme to help you remember the people involved in the plot:

Robert Catesby
Thomas Percy
Francis Tresham
Guy Fawkes

16.2 James I and Parliament

James firmly believed in the Divine Right of Kings, which declared that monarchs had their right to rule given to them by God. This attitude was to colour his dealings with Parliament.

- James himself proved to be an extravagant king who lived well and spent money unwisely. Consequently, he often had to ask Parliament for more funds.
- As King of England and Scotland, James had joined the two crowns in a personal union, but he also had an ambition to merge the two countries formally as one and declare himself the first King of Great Britain.
- When in 1604 he asked Parliament to approve this move and give him more money to finance the continuing war with Spain, Parliament refused and James ended the session.
- James started selling titles, such as peerages and knighthoods, and monopolies to companies. Parliament claimed that these actions were illegal.
- James called the Addled Parliament in 1614, but ended it only eight weeks later when it resisted his wishes to raise taxes.
- George Villiers, the Duke of Buckingham, rose to power through his friendship with the King. He advised James on his policies.
- James called a third Parliament in 1621, which he dissolved when Parliament tried to debate foreign policy and the proposed marriage between his son Charles and the daughter of the King of Spain, which the members did not support because she was Catholic.
- James' final Parliament, in 1624, was called in desperation to raise money. The Lord Treasurer, Sir Lionel Cranfield, was trying to stabilise the spending but Parliament had him removed from office. Parliament also agreed to give money for a war with Spain, which James did not support.

James I died in March 1625 and the throne passed to his son Charles.

16.3 Charles I and religion

Charles I was known to favour High Anglicanism, a Church that was Protestant but retained much of the splendour and ceremony of the Catholic Church.

- Charles married Henrietta Maria, the daughter of the King of France, who was Catholic. His marriage alarmed Parliament, who believed that he would move England towards Catholicism once more.
- Charles was a believer in the Divine Right of Kings and refused to allow people to question his decisions.
- In 1633, William Laud was appointed Archbishop of Canterbury. Laud was a High Anglican and upheld the role of bishops, allowed priests to wear vestments, and reintroduced old ceremonies and decorations into churches.
- Laud also persecuted Puritan radicals who opposed him. In 1637, three Puritans named William Prynne, Henry Burton and John Bastwick were tortured (they had their ears cut off) for speaking against him. The following year, a pamphleteer named 'Freeborn John' Lilburne was arrested.

The First Bishops' War

- In 1637, Charles and Laud introduced the new Prayer Book to Scotland and tried to give Scottish bishops the same powers as English ones. However, when the Prayer Book was first used in Scotland it led to riots.
- In 1638, the Scots signed a covenant declaring that they would defend their Protestantism. The following year, Charles sent an army to Scotland to enforce his changes.
- But in the struggle that followed, known as the First Bishops' War, the army was easily defeated by the Scots.
- In 1639, Parliament accused Laud of treason. He was tried in 1644, found guilty and executed the following year.

16.4 Charles I and Parliament

Charles I was already unpopular with many MPs because of his religious beliefs and his insistence on the Divine Right of Kings.

- Charles, like his father, was also a lavish spender. He was also under the influence of the Duke of Buckingham, who was unpopular with Parliament. Buckingham led a disastrous naval raid on the port of Cadiz in Spain and was then murdered by a disgruntled sailor.
- In 1627, in response to being offered only one-tenth of the money he requested, Charles dissolved Parliament. He therefore had to borrow the money from the people in a forced loan.
- In 1628, Charles attempted to increase the tax on certain goods. A group of MPs, led by John Pym, drew up the Petition of Right, which reminded the King that he had no right to raise taxes or take forced loans of his own accord.
- When Parliament presented Charles with the similar Three Resolutions the following year, he dissolved Parliament again. This time it was not called for eleven years, a period known as 'The Eleven Year Tyranny'.

Test yourself

Before moving on to the next chapter, make sure you can answer the following questions. The answers are at the back of the book.

1 When and where did James I refuse to dismiss the English bishops?

2 Why was the Addled Parliament of 1614 dissolved after eight weeks?

3 Which unpopular tax led to the trial of John Hampden?

4 Which five MPs did Charles I attempt to arrest in January 1642?

Civil War (1642–49) and the Interregnum (1649–60)

17.1 The English Civil War

The two sides in the English Civil War each formed an army.

- The Royalist army consisted of the old nobility, courtiers, Roman Catholics and Anglicans, and men from the country. They were known as Cavaliers.
- The Parliamentarian army consisted of the lesser gentry, merchants, Puritans and Presbyterians, and men from towns. They were known as Roundheads.

Charles and his army marched south to reclaim London. The Roundheads marched north and the two sides met at Edgehill in Warwickshire.

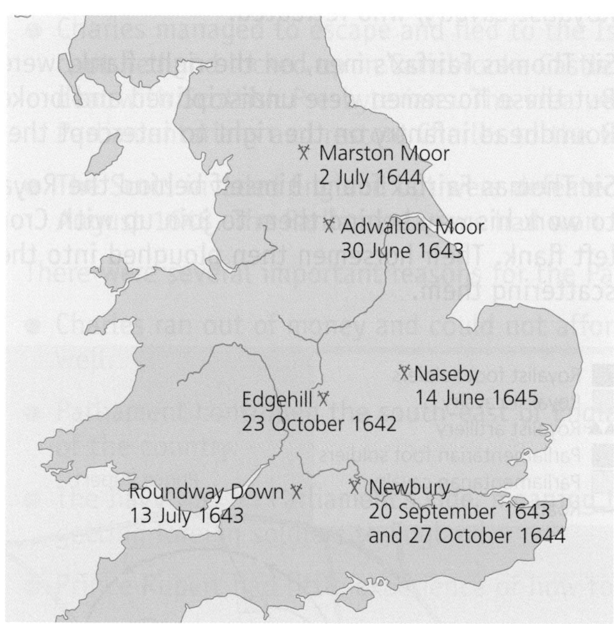

■ The key battles of the Civil War

- The Battle of Edgehill was fought on 23 October 1642. The Cavaliers were commanded by Charles' nephew Prince Rupert of the Rhine.
- The battle lasted three hours and ended in a stalemate, with no clear winner.
- Charles could have pushed on towards London, but he was unsure about whether he would face any resistance there. He therefore decided to wait.

In 1643, both sides won smaller battles but Charles still failed to march on London. Parliament made a pact with Scotland that drew them on to their side.

17.4 The trial and execution of Charles I

When Charles was arrested, the MPs debated what should be done with him. Most, like Cromwell, argued that they had tried to negotiate with the King before and that he had re-started the war by involving the Scots.

- On 6 December 1648, the Parliamentarian army surrounded the House of Commons and only allowed entry to those MPs who supported putting the King on trial. This was known as 'Pride's Purge'.
- The 240 MPs who were allowed entry to the House of Commons formed the Rump Parliament. They voted to put Charles on trial. The trial began in January 1649.

There were several charges against the King:

- He had abused his powers as King, ruling as a tyrant.
- He had declared war on his own people.
- He had attempted to turn the French and Irish against his own people.
- He had re-started the war by encouraging the Scots to invade.

Revision tip

You could try making up a phrase to help you remember the charges against Charles or perhaps use an illustration for each charge.

Charles claimed that the court had no right to put him on trial and refused to answer the charges.

- Eighty commissioners took part in the trial of Charles. The King was found guilty by 68 of the judges, 59 of whom signed his death warrant.
- The execution took place on the morning of 30 January 1649.

17.5 Cromwell and Parliament

With the King dead, Parliament declared England to be a Commonwealth. The House of Lords was abolished and a Council of State, consisting of MPs chosen from the Rump Parliament, was introduced. The real power to enforce the laws lay with the army, now commanded by Cromwell.

- The Rump Parliament did not prove to be effective and Cromwell was unable to bring about the reforms he really wanted.
- He dissolved the Rump Parliament on 20 April 1653. In its place, the new assembly became known as Barebone's Parliament. Cromwell wanted this to be a 'Parliament of the Saints' that would make laws according to strictly Puritan values.
- But the various groups in Barebone's Parliament were unable to work together. In December 1653, 40 frustrated MPs marched to Cromwell's home and handed their authority over to him.
- Barebone's Parliament was dissolved and, on 16 December 1653, Cromwell was appointed Lord Protector of England.

Lord Protector

- In 1655, England was divided into eleven districts and a Major-General was appointed in charge of keeping law and order in each one. A ten per cent tax, the decimation tax, was introduced to finance the Major-General's local armies in each district.
- Cromwell banned unlawful assemblies and the owning of weapons by known Royalists, and called for robbers and vagrants to be severely punished.
- While people were free to worship as they wished in private, new laws were introduced that attempted to make their way of life as Puritan as possible. Entertainment, dancing, singing and drinking alcohol were banned, as was the celebration of Christmas.
- In 1657, Cromwell gathered together his army leaders to discuss the drawing-up of a new constitution for England. The men were adamant that Cromwell should not declare himself a replacement for the monarch they had got rid of.
- Nonetheless, later that year, Cromwell was formally sworn in as Lord Protector in a magnificent ceremony, full of pomp and splendour that showed off his power.

Essay question

Try this sample essay question for yourself. A suggested answer is given at the back of the book.

Q Explain why there might have been opposition to the ceremony appointing Oliver Cromwell as Lord Protector in 1657. (30)

17.6 Ireland and Scotland

Ireland and Scotland had been ruled by the kings of England for many years. Now that the monarchy had been abolished, they declared themselves independent.

The conquest of Ireland

- Parliament feared that Charles I's son, also named Charles, might seek Irish support for his restoration to the throne.
- In 1649, Cromwell led a force to Ireland, occupied Dublin and attacked the town of Drogheda, killing around 3,500 Irish. In the southern town of Wexford, a further 1,500 Irish were killed in a similar assault.
- The Parliamentarians forced the Catholics to resettle in Connaught, in the west of Ireland. The lands that they left were divided up between Cromwell's men.

The conquest of Scotland

- In Scotland, Charles I's son (Charles Stuart) had been accepted as monarch and crowned King Charles II. This time, his supporters were not Catholics but Presbyterians.
- A Parliamentarian army defeated the Scots in battle at Dunbar in September 1650 and captured the city of Edinburgh.

18 Charles II (1660–85) and James II (1685–88)

18.1 Charles II

Charles II, known as the 'Merrie Monarch', was exactly the sort of king the Puritans hoped would never return to England.

- Charles lived well and spent lavishly. He is best known for his many mistresses, including the actress Nell Gwynn, and for fathering many illegitimate children.
- Although he had agreed to pardon those who had fought on the Parliamentarian side, Charles was determined to punish those involved in the death of his father. The surviving commissioners who had sentenced Charles I to death were put on trial for regicide and either imprisoned or executed.
- The corpses of some Republican figures who had already died – including Oliver Cromwell himself – were exhumed, publicly hanged and then decapitated. Their heads were placed upon poles.
- The Parliament that elected to restore Charles to the throne was called the Convention Parliament. It repealed all the Acts of Parliament passed during the Interregnum.
- The next session, the Cavalier Parliament, allowed the King to regain some of the rights that had been taken from his father.
- Charles regained control of the army and Parliament agreed to give the army a sum of money every year to support it.
- Later, the members of the Cavalier Parliament began to split into two groups. One group – the Tory Party – was strongly supportive of the King. The other – the Whig Party – wanted to restrict the King's power.

18.2 Plague and fire

- In 1665, bubonic plague returned to England and took hold in London.
- A member of the King's government named Samuel Pepys kept a diary during the years 1660–69. It is a valuable source of information on the effects of the outbreak on the people of London.
- People living in infected houses were quarantined for a month under the guard of watchmen. The infected houses were marked with a red cross. Women were employed to keep track of the deaths and record the number of victims.
- The number of deaths in London peaked during August, when the weather was hottest. As it grew colder, the rate of victims dropped.

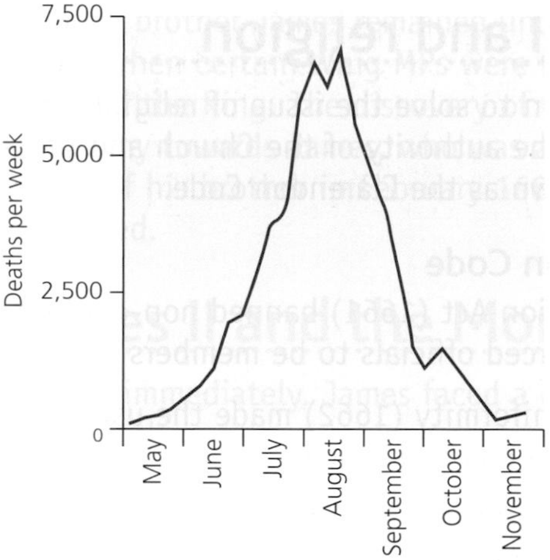

■ The Great Plague (1665)

The Great Fire of London (1666)

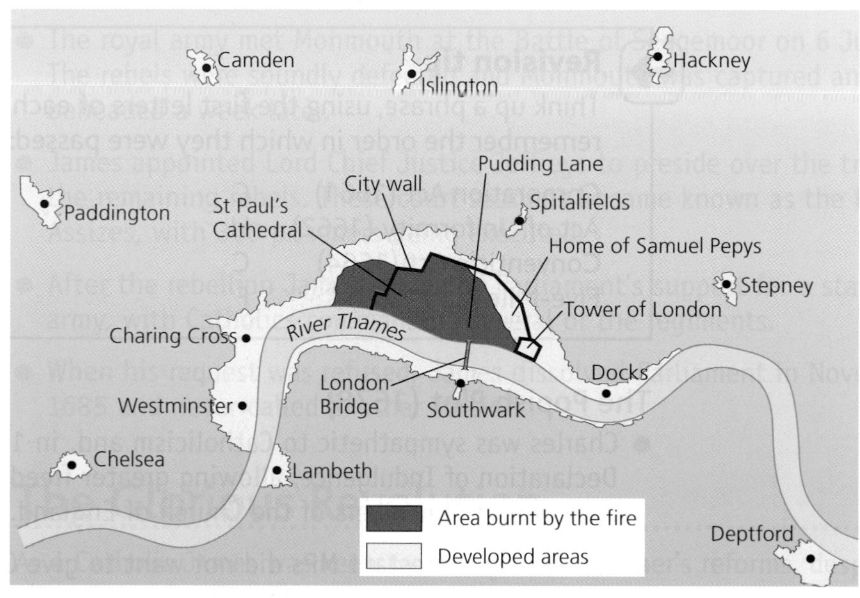

- In the early hours of 2 September 1666, a fire broke out in Thomas Farynor's bakery in Pudding Lane. It quickly spread through the neighbouring wooden houses.
- Fanned by strong easterly winds that drove the flames westwards, the fire lasted five days.
- There were very few human casualties, but the fire engulfed three-quarters of the land within the city walls. Thousands of people were made homeless or lost their trade.
- When the city was rebuilt, the streets were made wider and buildings were constructed with brick and stone rather than wood. Sir Christopher Wren designed the new St Paul's Cathedral and a monument to the fire that stands close to where Pudding Lane once was.

Evidence question

You may be asked to answer an evidence question on the Plague and the Fire of London. Refer to the guidance on page xi and make sure that you practise answering these questions.

- James fled to France the following month. The crown was offered to Mary as James' daughter, but William refused to allow this unless he could rule jointly with his wife. They were crowned King William III and Queen Mary II in April 1689.

Revision tip

Try using a sketch or, perhaps, a flow chart to help you remember the events of the Glorious Revolution. Remember to use different colours to help you remember the different points.

18.6 Culture and science

The reigns of the Tudors and Stuarts brought great advances in the arts and science. Many famous artists, writers, scientists and philosophers of the period produced works that are still studied and enjoyed today.

Artists

- Hans Holbein (c.1497–1543) was the most important court painter of his time, producing famous portraits of Henry VIII and Edward VI.
- Nicholas Hilliard (c.1547–1619) was a specialist in producing miniatures.
- Anthony van Dyck (1599–1641) was the main court painter during the reign of Charles I.

Writers

- William Shakespeare (1564–1616) was the most famous and influential playwright of his age, and 38 of his plays survive today. Shakespeare and a group of players called the King's Men built their own theatre called the Globe.
- Edmund Spenser (1552–99) is regarded as one of the greatest English poets. He was particularly popular with Elizabeth I and wrote an allegory, *The Faerie Queene*, in her honour.
- Christopher Marlowe (1564–93) was a playwright as popular as Shakespeare during his lifetime, but died young after a drunken brawl in a tavern.
- John Bunyan (1628–88) was a non-conformist who was imprisoned for preaching without a licence. While in prison, he wrote a famous allegory called *The Pilgrim's Progress*.

Scientists

- Francis Bacon (1561–1626) encouraged the empirical method, which argued that scientific knowledge was gained by the observation of behaviour rather than the discussion of possible theories.
- William Harvey (1578–1657) discovered the method of circulation by which blood is pumped around the body.
- In 1660 Charles II set up the Royal Society, which provided a place for scientists to carry out their work without fear of attack by the Church. The following scientists were all members of the Society.
- Isaac Newton (1642–1727) is known as the founder of modern science. He famously studied gravity and drew up several laws of motion.

- Christopher Wren (1632–1723) was an architect who rebuilt London after the Great Fire of 1666.
- Edmond Halley (1656–1742) was an astronomer who discovered Halley's Comet and helped to map much of the universe that is visible from Earth.

Revision tip

You could use pictures to help you remember what each of the scientists contributed. Think what you would draw for each of the table entries below.

Francis Bacon	
William Harvey	
Isaac Newton	
Christopher Wren	
Edmond Halley	

Philosophers

- Thomas Hobbes (1588–1679) argued that people are naturally wicked and unfit to hold positions of authority. He therefore believed that monarchy was the best form of government.
- John Locke (1632–1704) argued that people are born as a 'blank slate' (*tabula rasa*) without ideas, and that their experiences in life form their way of thinking. He did not support the idea of monarchy.

★ Make sure you know

★ The early events of the reign of Charles II.

★ The events of the Great Plague of 1665 and the Great Fire of London of 1666.

★ The religious views of Charles II, and the events and consequences of the Popish Plot.

★ The early events of the reign of James II and the Monmouth Rebellion.

★ The religious views of James II, and the events and consequences of the Glorious Revolution.

★ The work of the most famous artists, writers, scientists and philosophers of the period.

- In 1722, a Jacobite plot was discovered in which Francis Atterbury, a leading Tory, was implicated. Walpole convinced people that all Tories were Jacobite rebels and the Whigs became more popular.

20.3 Trade and the empire

During the reign of George I, Britain's trade routes across the world became established.

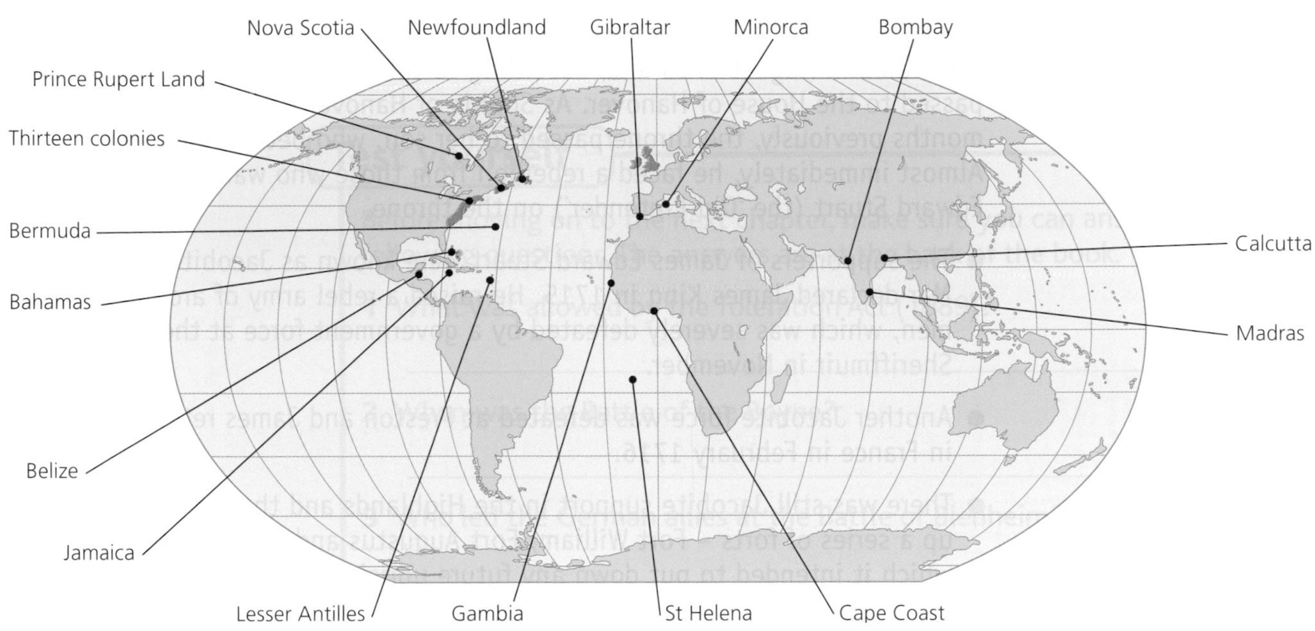

■ Britain's Empire at the time of George I

- By 1727, Britain owned colonies in America, the West Indies and parts of Canada. There were also trading bases in India and Gibraltar.
- Trade routes between Britain, Africa and America formed a system called the Triangular Trade. The British took manufactured goods to Africa and sold them in exchange for slaves. The slaves were then transported to America and exchanged for valuable commodities, such as tobacco, cotton, sugar and coffee, which were then shipped back to Britain.

Produce to Europe

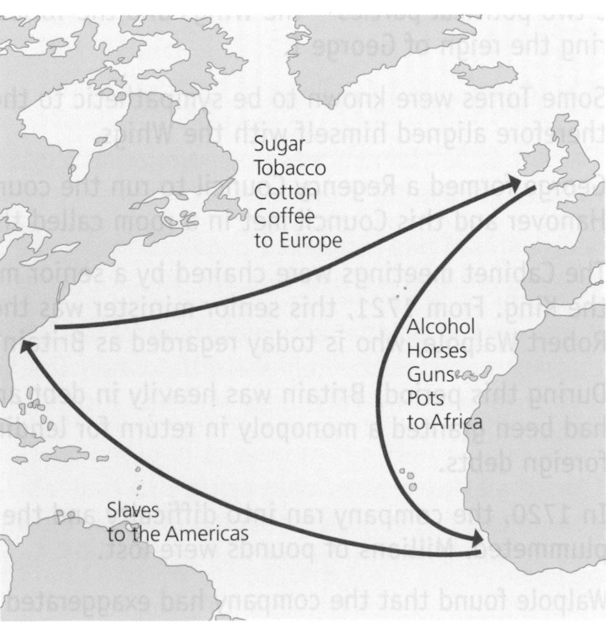

■ The Triangular Trade

Goods to Africa

Slaves to the West Indies

George I died while on a visit to Hanover in June 1727. He was succeeded by his son, who became George II.

20.4 George II and war with Europe

The War of Jenkins' Ear (1739–42)

- British success in gaining an empire had been greatly resented by Spain. In 1729, Spain signed the Treaty of Seville, which gave Spaniards the right to board British ships sailing in Spanish waters.
- In 1731 Spaniards boarded a British ship captained by Robert Jenkins, who had his ear cut off in the ensuing fight.
- Several years later, Jenkins displayed his preserved ear to Parliament and the outrage it caused led to war being declared on Spain.
- In 1739 the British captured the Spanish town of Porto Bello in Panama, but any further attempts to take Spanish strongholds failed. Robert Walpole was forced to resign in 1742.

The War of the Austrian Succession (1742–48)

- In 1740, the Emperor of Austria, Charles VI, died and left the throne to his daughter Maria Theresa. This succession was disputed by Frederick II of Prussia.
- Prussia was supported by France, who threatened to invade Hanover in 1742, bringing George – and Britain – into the conflict. George personally led an army of English and Hanoverians at the Battle of Dettingen on 27 June 1743 and defeated the French.
- France then raided the British fortified towns in Maine in 1745. A combined force of British and American colonials captured the French fortification of Fort Louisbourg in Nova Scotia.
- Both sides signed the Treaty of Aix-la-Chapelle in 1748, ending the war.

20.5 The 1745 Jacobite Rebellion

By 1745, James Edward Stuart had a 24-year-old son, Charles, who was to enter folk legend as Bonnie Prince Charlie.

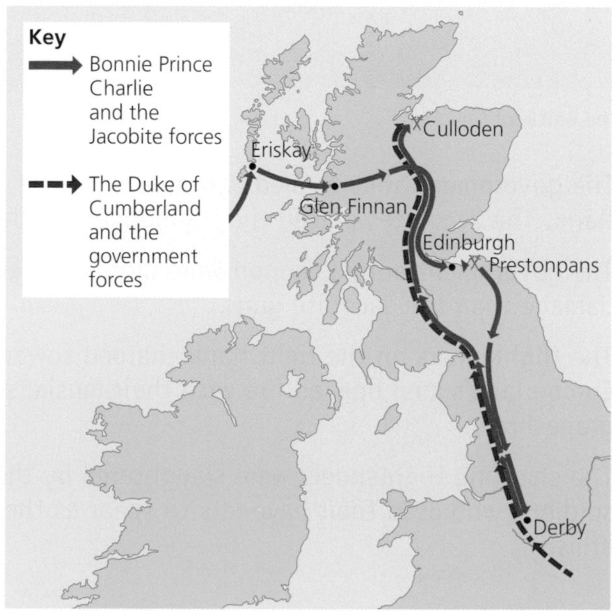

- Charles landed with a small group of followers on the island of Eriskay, off the west coast of Scotland, in July 1745. He gained the support of several Scottish clans, raising an army of over 4,000.
- The Jacobites defeated a government army at the Battle of Prestonpans on 21 September 1745.
- Charles crossed the border into England, confident that English Jacobites would support him. But this did not happen and, by the time they reached Derby, Charles' advisors persuaded him to turn back.
- Back in Scotland, Charles tried to capture Stirling Castle. The Jacobites managed to defeat another government army at the Battle of Falkirk on 17 January 1746.
- George II asked his son William, Duke of Cumberland, to go after the Jacobites. The two sides met on Culloden Moor, near Inverness, on 16 April 1746.

The Battle of Culloden, 16 April 1746

- The Jacobites were short of food and supplies, and expected reinforcements from France which had not yet arrived.
- Charles and his highest commander, Lord George Murray, disagreed over when and where to fight. Charles refused to listen to Murray's advice to withdraw from Culloden and fight elsewhere.

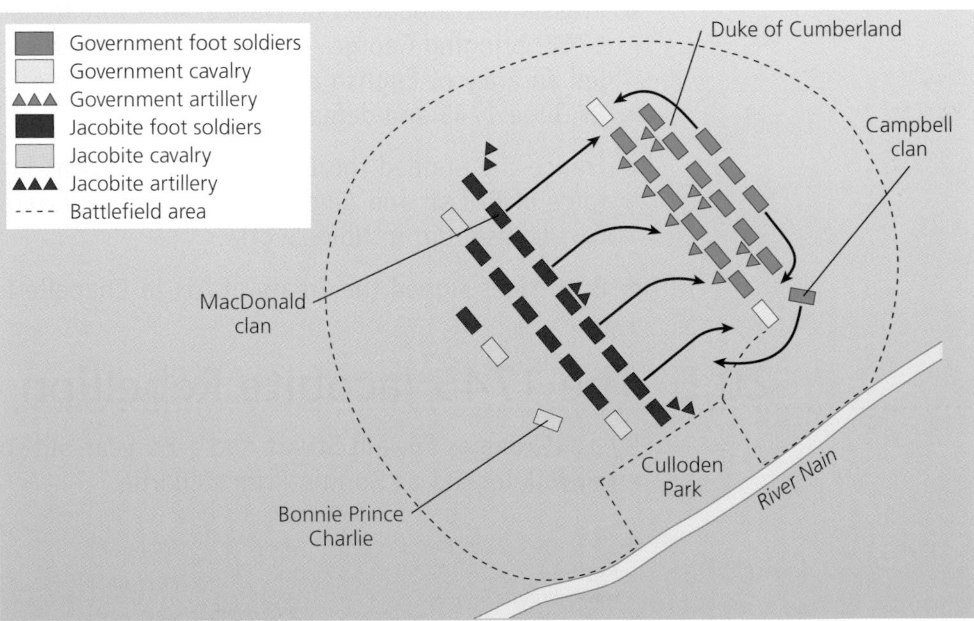

■ The Battle of Culloden

- The government army formed two lines with the cavalry placed on each flank. The Jacobites placed the Highlanders in the front line.
- The government army's cannon were more accurate and caused more damage than the Jacobite guns.
- The Highlanders on the right flank charged towards the government army. Cumberland's men opened fire with their muskets and cannon loaded with grapeshot.
- The charging Highlanders were slaughtered by the well-trained government soldiers, who used their bayonets to spear as the enemy raised their sword arms.

- Charles and the Jacobites retreated. Around 1,000 Jacobites were lost, compared with only 50 government soldiers.
- For the next three months, Cumberland's troops rounded up 3,500 men and executed more than 100.
- Charles escaped to the Isle of Skye, with the help of a local girl named Flora Macdonald. He reached France and lived in exile for the rest of his life.

Essay question

Try this sample essay question for yourself. A suggested answer is given at the back of the book.

Q Explain why the 1745 Jacobite Rebellion was not successful. (30)

★ Make sure you know

★ The events and consequences of the 1715 Jacobite Rebellion.

★ The development of the political party system and position of Robert Walpole during the reign of George I.

★ The reasons for the establishment and growth of the British Empire.

★ The events of the War of Jenkins' Ear and the War of the Austrian Succession.

★ The events and consequences of the 1745 Jacobite Rebellion.

Test yourself

Make sure you can answer the following questions. The answers are at the back of the book.

1 Which three government forts were built in Scotland after the 1715 Jacobite Rebellion?

____

2 Sales of shares in which company caused a stock market crash in 1720?

____

3 By which treaty were the Spanish allowed to board British vessels in Spanish waters?

____

4 Who led the English and Hanoverian army at the Battle of Dettingen?

____

5 Which Jacobite commander advised Bonnie Prince Charlie not to fight at Culloden?

____

PART C
BRITAIN AND EMPIRE 1750–1914

21 The Seven Years' War

21.1 Background

- By 1750, significant communities of British settlers existed on the eastern side of what is now the United States of America. The French had made settlements north of this in what is now Canada.
- In the early 1750s, the French tried to expand their settlements southwards and westwards, into the British colonies of Virginia, New York and Georgia, and built a row of forts along the Appalachian Mountains.
- In 1754, George Washington, a young officer in the Virginia militia, attempted to capture Fort Duquesne from the French, but was defeated. This incident provoked war between the two nations, and both Britain and France sent troops to the colonies to reinforce their armies there.
- In 1755, General Edward Braddock made another attempt to capture Fort Duquesne with more than 2,000 men. But Braddock had no experience of fighting in dense forests. The British were ambushed and defeated by the French and a tribe of Native Americans at the Battle of Monongahela River.

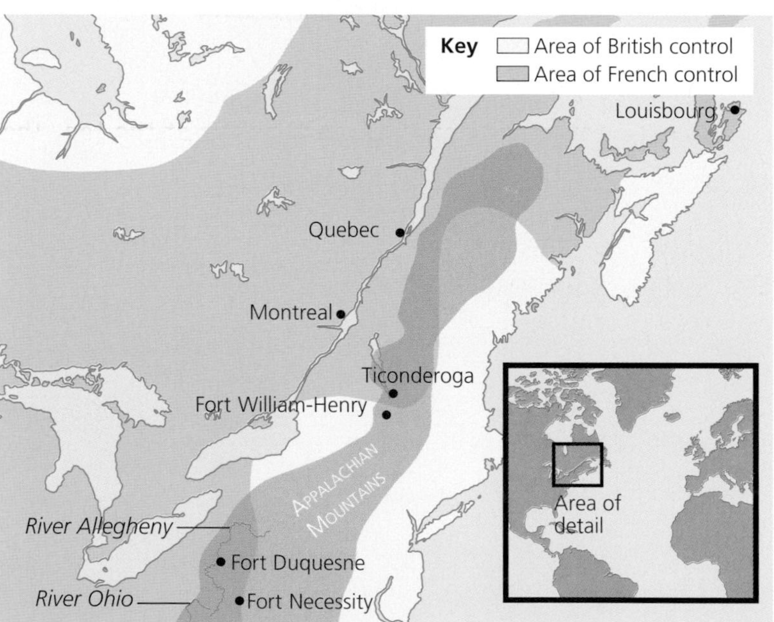

■ North America and the Seven Years' War

21.2 William Pitt the Elder

- William Pitt was a Member of Parliament who opposed the Duke of Newcastle's government and the way they were conducting the war. He gained support from his fellow MPs and, despite the refusal of King George II to appoint him Prime Minister, became Secretary of State in 1757 and was placed in charge of the British campaign.

- Pitt believed that the navy was crucial to victory. Under the command of Admiral George Anson the navy blockaded ports in France, preventing their ships from supplying French troops in the colonies.
- Pitt also believed that the French needed to be defeated in the colonies rather than in Europe. However, he gave money to King Frederick the Great of Prussia, encouraging him to keep fighting the French at home.
- Meanwhile, in the colonies, the French captured the British Fort William-Henry. Despite French promises to allow the British troops to leave peacefully, 300 soldiers were attacked and killed by their Native American allies.
- The British were outraged by this incident and formed a well-trained brigade of light infantry to launch an offensive against the French. They managed to capture the French forts one by one. Fort Duquesne was destroyed and the site renamed Fort Pitt.

21.3 Wolfe and the fall of Quebec

- Major-General James Wolfe had proved his expertise with nearly twenty years' service in the army. He was popular, with an excellent reputation, but his radical ideas were regarded with suspicion by some. Pitt instructed him to take the city of Quebec, the capital of French Canada.
- Quebec was built at the top of a steep cliff and defended by General Montcalm with 16,000 men. Wolfe had fewer than 10,000 but was supported by a huge navy. These ships sailed up the St Lawrence River in June 1759 and set their guns on Quebec.
- The French planned to hold out until the river froze in the winter. But, on the night of 12 September, Wolfe led a small band of men up the cliff side, overpowering the French militia at the top. The path was cleared for the rest of Wolfe's army to follow.
- The Battle of the Plains of Abraham was fought the next day. Both commanders, Wolfe and Montcalm, were killed, along with 58 British and 500 French troops. The French were routed and forced back into the city of Quebec, which fell to the British five days later.

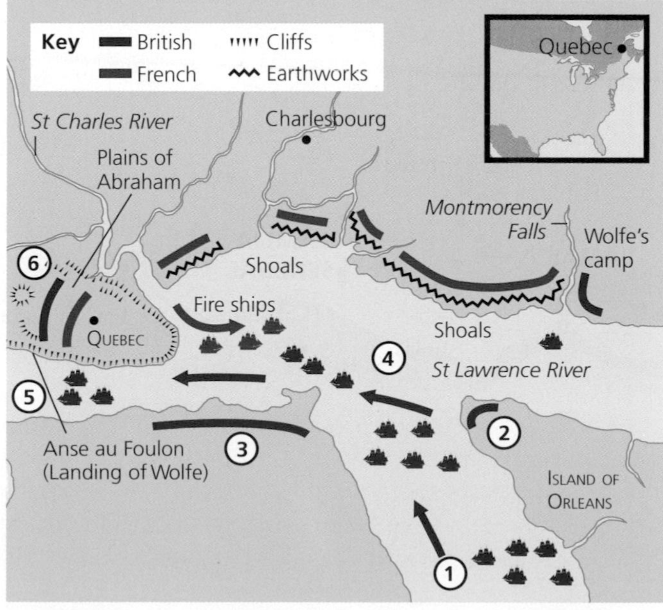

■ Map of Quebec showing the sequence of events during the siege

Essay question

Try this sample essay question for yourself. A suggested answer is given at the back of the book.

Q Explain the importance of the role of James Wolfe in the Battle of the Plains of Abraham. (30)

21.4 British victories and the end of the campaign

- In the winter of 1760 the French, seeing that the frozen St Lawrence River had forced the British fleet to leave, attempted to retake Quebec. The British managed to hold out until the spring, when the river thawed and their ships were able to return.
- In September 1760, the French surrendered the city of Montreal to General Amherst. The French now no longer had a foothold in Canada.
- The British divided up the old French Canada into smaller colonies and took over the French-owned lands in the West Indies.
- King George II died in October 1760. His grandson, now George III, wanted to end the war, and began to take greater control of the government.
- Pitt resigned as Secretary of State when he could not persuade the government to launch a surprise attack on Spain, which was threatening to join the war, in 1761. Spain did join the war the following year but Britain was able to seize its colonies in Cuba and the Philippines.
- The war ended and a peace treaty, the Peace of Paris, was agreed in 1763. Britain kept control of Canada, but many of the West Indies islands were returned to France. Cuba and the Philippines were returned to Spain, but Britain took control of Florida.

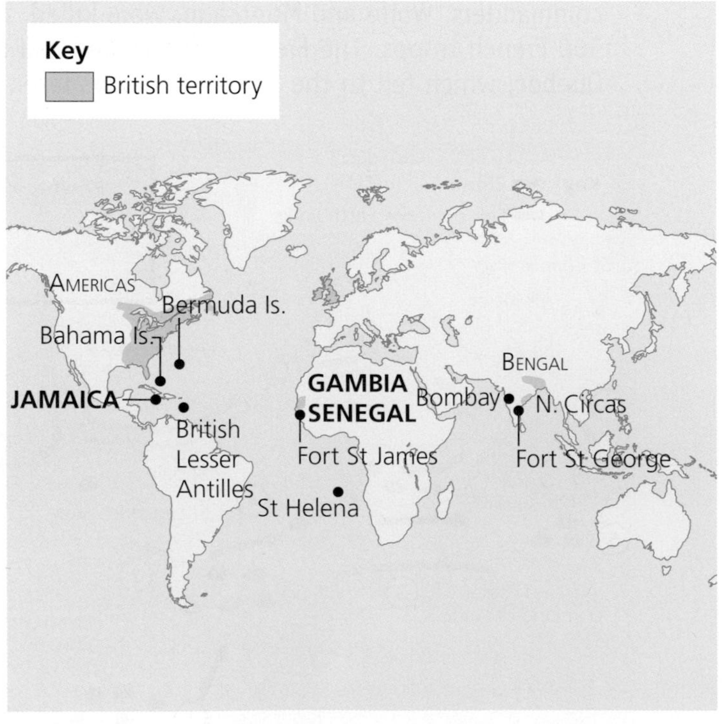

Revision tip

Flash cards are good for testing your knowledge about the important generals and politicians in the Seven Years' War. For example, draw the face of William Pitt (or just his name if you prefer) on one side of a card; on the other side write down his characteristics, accomplishments and failures. See how many of the key points you can remember just from looking at the face side of each card.

You might ask a friend to test you with the flash cards to make it more interesting.

★ Make sure you know

- ★ The events forming the background to the Seven Years' War.
- ★ The key events in the career of William Pitt the Elder.
- ★ The reasons for Wolfe's victory and the events of the fall of Quebec.
- ★ The events surrounding the end of the Seven Years' War.

Test yourself ✓

Before moving on to the next chapter, make sure you can answer the following questions. The answers are at the back of the book.

1 Two attempts were made to capture which French fort in 1754 and 1755?

______________________________ ☐

2 Which European monarch did Pitt the Elder encourage to fight the French in Europe?

______________________________ ☐

3 Who was the French commander during the Battle of the Plains of Abraham?

______________________________ ☐

4 Which peace treaty ended the Seven Years' War in 1763?

______________________________ ☐

22 The American Rebellion and World War

22.1 Background

The Seven Years' War placed Britain in £140 million worth of debt. It was decided that its colonies should take their fair share of the burden in paying it off.

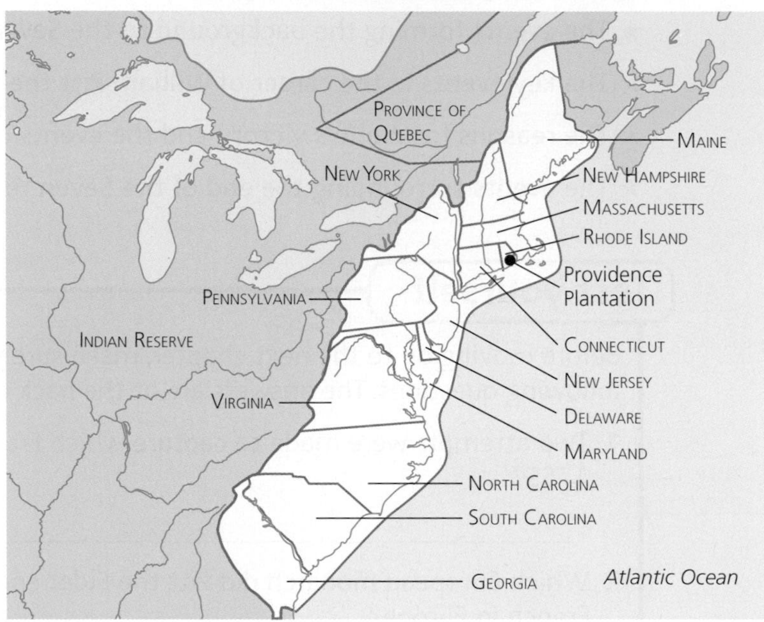

■ The American colonies in 1770

The Stamp Tax

- The Stamp Tax was introduced in 1765. Legal documents, newspapers, playing cards and dice now had to bear a stamp that could only be bought from the government.
- A rebel group from Boston, Massachusetts, called the Sons of Liberty, used threats of violence against anyone trying to sell the stamps. They called for a boycott of British goods, at a time when the government had banned the colonies from importing from anywhere else. The trade in goods smuggled in from France and Spain began to grow.
- The rebels declared that the people could only be represented by those they had themselves chosen, and no taxes could be imposed upon them from outside their own colony. They took up the slogan 'No taxation without representation'.
- These protests forced the government to repeal the Stamp Tax in 1766.

The Boston Massacre

- In 1767, the Chancellor of the Exchequer, Charles Townshend, passed the Townshend Duties, a set of taxes on certain goods such as tea, glass, paper and paint.

- A Boston rebel named Samuel Adams persuaded the Massachusetts Assembly to declare the Townshend Duties illegal. The British then sent troops to enforce the taxes. Those who supported Adams called themselves 'Patriots', while those on the British side were termed 'Loyalists'.
- On the night of 5 March 1770, a group of Boston locals were taunting the British soldiers guarding the Customs House. A shot was fired and the soldiers, believing they were under attack, fired into the crowd. In all, five were killed and several more injured.
- Despite the soldiers being found not guilty of murder, the Patriots used the incident to stir up more anti-British feeling.

The Boston Tea Party

- The Townshend Duties were eventually repealed until the only tax remaining was on the import of tea.
- In order to support the East India Company, which was in financial trouble, in 1773 the government decided to sell tea to the colonies at vastly reduced prices. This was both to help the company and to allow the government to collect the import tax as well.
- The Patriots were naturally opposed to this last remaining tax. On the night of 16 December 1773, about 200 Patriots, disguised as Native Americans, went to Boston Harbour and boarded three ships with cargoes of tea waiting to be unloaded. The crates of tea were smashed and the contents thrown over the side.
- The government's reaction was to pass the Coercive Acts the following year. These laws closed the port of Boston, reduced the power of the colonial assembly there, and placed Massachusetts under the military control of General Gage.
- Representatives of Patriots from each colony met at the Continental Congress in September 1774. They agreed to boycott British goods and petitioned King George III with a list of complaints, which was ignored.

? Evidence question

You may be asked to answer an evidence question on the causes of the American War of Independence. Refer to the guidance on page xi and make sure that you practise answering these questions.

22.2 The outbreak of war

General Gage did not expect the militia in Massachusetts to give up easily, and made plans to capture their arms store at Concord.

The Battles of Lexington and Concord

- British soldiers, led by Major Pitcairn, arrived in Lexington at dawn on 19 April 1775, to find a group of armed militiamen parading on the village green. Pitcairn ordered the men to lay down their weapons and disperse, which some attempted to do.
- Then a shot was fired, possibly from the local tavern. The British fired two volleys at the militia and then charged forward with their bayonets. Eight militiamen were killed and ten wounded.

- The British marched on to Concord, where they destroyed the rebels' arms store and set fire to some buildings. Four hundred militiamen began to fire on the British, forcing them back along the road towards Lexington.
- The Patriots dispersed at Lexington when British reinforcements arrived. Forty-nine militiamen were killed; the British lost 73 men and many more were wounded.

The Battle of Bunker Hill

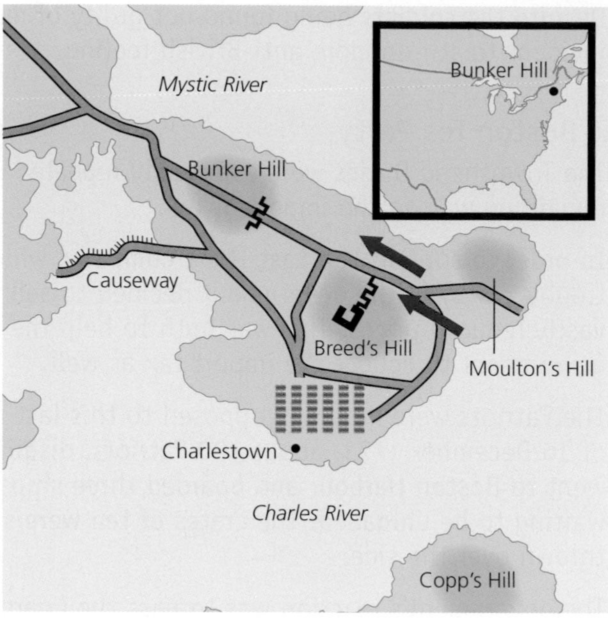

■ The British attack on the American position on Breed's Hill; the American rebels were threatening British shipping in the harbour

- Once the British had got back to Boston, thousands of militiamen had surrounded the city, digging trenches and trapping General Gage's forces inside.
- On 17 June 1775, the British began to bomb the trenches and earthworks on nearby Bunker Hill, at the entrance to the Charlestown Peninsula. They were commanded by General William Howe.
- The British took three attempts, but eventually managed to overrun the rebel defences and secure the peninsula. However, they suffered heavy losses: over 200 killed and 800 injured.

George Washington and the British

- The Patriots held another Continental Congress in May 1775, at which George Washington was named as the commander of the forces surrounding Boston.
- Washington was an experienced militiaman, and was well liked and respected. He was not a great military tactician but was able to organise supplies and reinforcements to keep his army going, even through the toughest times.
- The colonies rarely agreed on anything and had no established system of government, or a professional army. It was thought that Britain, with her superior army and navy, could easily defeat the rebels.

- However, neither side had universal support. Two-thirds of the population of the colonies either supported the British or did not care either way. Many in Britain did not like the idea of fighting people they regarded as fellow Britons, and were concerned that the war would be expensive.

22.3 The early war

1776

- In March 1776, the British left Boston and the Patriots began to invade other colonies in order to provoke further rebellion. Montreal was captured but retaken by the British in May 1776.
- On 4 July 1776, the delegates at the Continental Congress signed their Declaration of Independence. They wanted to show that they were a united group of independent states fighting a war against Britain, rather than a dispersed collection of rebels. They hoped that this would encourage Britain's enemies to join their side.
- The British were reinforced by friendly German troops and, in July 1776, General Howe led an assault on New York. He drove George Washington out of the city and when winter came, not expecting further fighting, he stood down his troops until the warmer spring weather.
- Washington's men began an assault on Christmas Day, defeating British and allied troops at Trenton and Princeton in New Jersey.

1777

- The British General Burgoyne proposed to cut off the New England colonies from the rest by marching his army south along the Hudson River. In doing so he managed to capture Ticonderoga, Hubbardton and Fort Edward.
- Meanwhile, General Howe attacked Philadelphia, the apparent capital of the colonies, by sea, and successfully captured the city.
- Seven thousand colonials, under the command of General Gates, built entrenchments at Bemis Heights, Saratoga, in order to stop the British march southward. Gates was aided by two notable colonels, Daniel Morgan and Benedict Arnold.

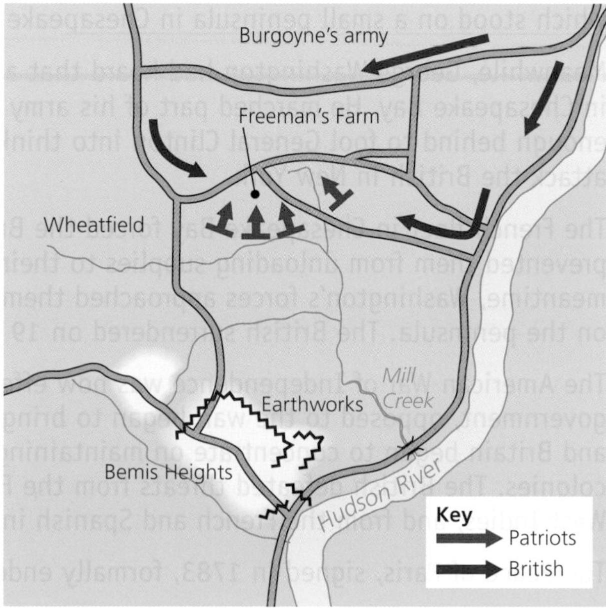

■ The Battle of Bemis Heights

23 The French Revolution and the Napoleonic Wars

23.1 The French Revolution

France was Britain's main colonial rival, and wanted to expand and maintain its empire, but there was widespread discontent among the French people.

- France was bankrupt after supporting the Patriots in the American War of Independence.
- The poor and the middle classes had to pay taxes while the nobility, which controlled the military and the Church, did not have to.
- People did not receive fair trials or have access to the law. The system was run by the aristocracy, who had been chosen not because of their ability, but by who their ancestors were.
- Prices were rising due to poor harvests and people were starving, unable to grow or buy produce.

Course of the revolution

- Parliament (the Estates General) met in 1789 and discussed these problems. They concluded that the monarchy and aristocracy were at the root of a corrupt system.
- Riots broke out in Paris and the Bastille, a royal fortress, was taken over by the mob. They forced the nobles and clergy out of Parliament, which now renamed itself the National Assembly.
- Tribunals were set up against those who were suspected of being connected with the old regime. King Louis XVI and Queen Marie Antoinette were executed in 1793.
- Other European countries supported the aims of the revolution but were horrified by the violence in France. Leaders worried that the idea would spread to their countries.
- To stop the spread of revolution, France was invaded by Prussia and Austria. The French raised huge armies which defeated the invaders.
- In 1799 the army took over the Assembly, disbanded it and set up General Napoleon Bonaparte as Emperor of France. He wiped out the old corruption and supported fair principles but effectively ruled as a king.

23.2 William Pitt the Younger

- William Pitt, the son of Pitt the Elder (see page 116), became Prime Minister aged just 24 and served for seventeen years.
- He improved Britain's economy after the American War of Independence by reforming the tax system, clamping down on smuggling, and removing corrupt government officials.

- The British were particularly worried that revolutionary ideas would spread from France, and radicals in Britain were already supporting this. The government instead gave support to the loyalists, who opposed the radicals.
- Pitt suspended the right of *habeas corpus* – the rule that people cannot be arrested and held indefinitely without a trial. The government also outlawed large public meetings and trade unions.
- Pitt also persuaded other countries to fight by promising money and arms if they declared war on France.
- His military tactic was to use the British navy to blockade the French in their own ports, and to seize the French colonies so that Britain could grow wealthier from an expanded empire.
- The French ignored the British navy and, knowing that they had a large army, instead provoked countries such as Spain, Prussia and Austria into a land war.

Essay question

Try this sample essay question for yourself. A suggested answer is given at the back of the book.

Q Explain whether William Pitt the Younger was successful as Prime Minister. (30)

23.3 Horatio Nelson

- Nelson proved himself an able military commander at battles such as St Vincent in 1797, where he showed remarkable bravery. He had confidence in the navy, and in battle sought to fight as aggressively as possible.
- He inspired loyalty among his crew and shared his plans willingly with them, trusting them to act appropriately in battle. This was a technique that became known as 'the Nelson Touch'.
- Nelson became notorious for his affair with the wife of the British ambassador in Naples, Lady Emma Hamilton, who was attracted by his heroism. Despite being already married, he had a daughter, Horatia, by her.
- In 1798, Nelson sought to destroy the French fleet that accompanied Napoleon Bonaparte in the Mediterranean. He drew them into an overnight battle at Aboukir Bay in Egypt, and destroyed eleven of France's thirteen most important ships.
- In 1800, Sweden, Norway, Denmark, Russia and Prussia formed an alliance against the British. Nelson drew the Danish fleet into battle the following year, although he was under the command of Admiral Sir Hyde Parker. When Parker signalled to retreat, Nelson supposedly placed his telescope on his blind eye and said 'I really do not see the signal'. His tactics paid off and Denmark surrendered.

23.6 The Waterloo campaign

- Napoleon forced the Anglo-Dutch and Prussian armies to retreat during some skirmishes before the Battle of Waterloo. On the evening of 17 June 1815, Wellington lined his army up on the Mont St Jean ridge, blocking the road to Brussels. He hoped that he could hold out against the French for long enough to be reinforced by Blücher's army.
- The French army opened fire at 1pm the following day. Napoleon intended to break the Anglo-Dutch line and force them away from the advancing Prussians. His initial advance was thrown back by the British cavalry, who nonetheless suffered heavy losses.

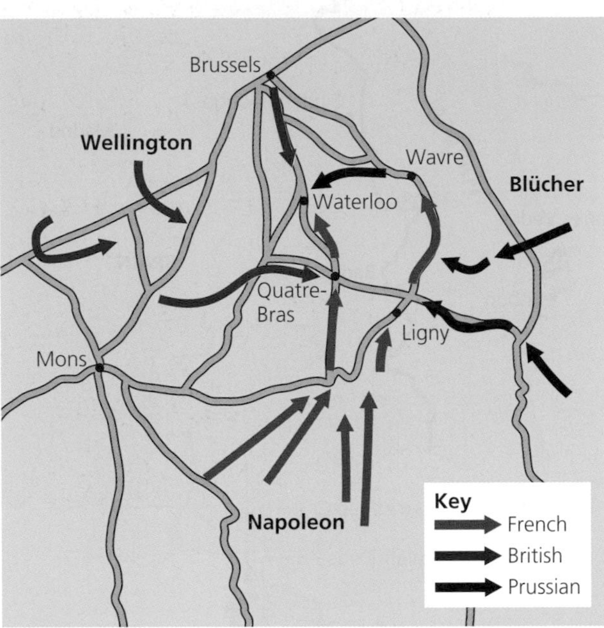

■ A map of the battlefield of Waterloo on the morning of 18 June 1815

- Wellington reorganised his troops on the ridge but this was mistaken for a retreat. The French Marshal Ney sent his cavalry to attack the centre of the British line at 4pm. But instead of retreating in disarray, the British remained in well-disciplined squares.
- By 6pm the French had nearly broken the Anglo-Dutch line. Napoleon could have ordered his elite units, the Imperial Guard, to attack, but he was distracted by the Prussian advances on his right. The French cavalry was unable to advance further without infantry support.
- The Imperial Guard was finally sent in one hour later. As they charged up the ridge, British soldiers who had been lying on the ground got up and fired at point-blank range. As the French retreated, Wellington ordered the whole of his army to advance.
- Napoleon fled the battlefield, but surrendered to the British and, this time, was sent into exile in St Helena in the South Atlantic, where he died in 1821.

Revision tip

Creating a set of index cards might help you remember key facts about the French Revolution and the Napoleonic Wars. Create one or two index cards for each sub-topic: the course of the revolution, William Pitt's foreign policy, Trafalgar and Waterloo. On one side of each card, write out all the big questions you might need to answer; on the other side write the answers to the questions.

You might also want to create index cards about Horatio Nelson and Arthur Wellesley.

★ Make sure you know

- ★ The key causes and events of the French Revolution.
- ★ The key events in the lives and careers of William Pitt the Younger, Horatio Nelson and Arthur Wellesley.
- ★ The key events of the Trafalgar campaign.
- ★ The key events of the Waterloo campaign.

Test yourself

Before moving on to the next chapter, make sure you can answer the following questions. The answers are at the back of the book.

1 Which new name did the French Parliament give itself after 1789?

____

2 What is the name of the rule of law which holds that people cannot be arrested and held indefinitely without a trial?

____

3 At which Mediterranean battle in 1798 did Nelson destroy most of the French ships?

____

4 Nelson was hit and killed by a musket ball fired from which French ship?

____

5 At which battle in 1812 did Arthur Wellesley force the French out of Spain?

____

6 Where was Napoleon Bonaparte exiled to in 1812?

____

25 The Agricultural and Industrial Revolutions

25.1 The Agricultural Revolution

Background

- In the early part of the eighteenth century most British farming worked on the 'open field' system. The land surrounding a village was jointly owned by all the farmers, who all farmed the same crop on each shared field. The crops were grown in rotation, and every three years a field was left fallow, or unseeded, in order for the soil to recover its nutrients.
- On land unsuitable for crops, livestock would be reared. They could also graze on common ground where wood could also be gathered for fires. These animals would be slaughtered in the autumn and the meat stored over winter.
- Word began to spread about new methods of farming that produced higher yields and a better quality of produce.

New methods

- A new type of crop-rotation system, where crops such as turnips or clover were sown during the fallow year, was introduced in the 1730s. The livestock could eat this produce and be kept alive over the winter.
- In the 1760s, Robert Bakewell experimented with the selective breeding of cattle and sheep. He only allowed males and females with good characteristics to mate. This produced sheep with both good quality meat and good quality fleeces, and cows that did not have to be fed as much. Bakewell's animals were hired out to other farmers for breeding with their own stock.
- A writer named Arthur Young produced a book of new ideas, *A Course of Experimental Agriculture*, that became popular among farmers. Young gained a government post and advised farmers on the best agricultural practices.

New technology

- In 1701, Jethro Tull invented the seed drill, which planted the corn in neat rows. Then the Rotherham plough, which could be operated by one man and fewer horses, appeared in 1730.
- Other new inventions to make farmers' lives easier included the iron ploughshare, the reaping machine and the threshing gin.
- Farmers were keen to use the new techniques, but they would only work if a farmer used the same crops every year. The old system of land use would not allow it, so increasingly land became 'enclosed' – that is, a farmer had his portion of land fenced off and permanently allocated to him. This was a complicated procedure and it did not work for all farmers, especially those who were suspicious of the new methods.

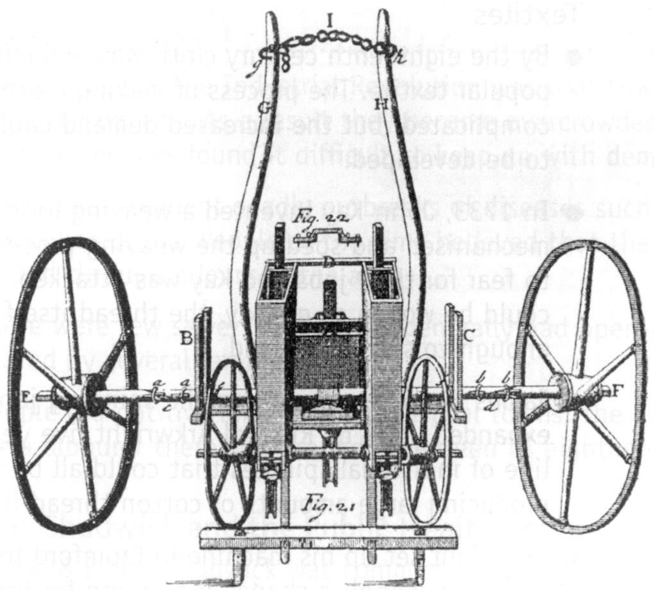

■ Jethro Tull's seed drill, 1701

- Farming families began to move out of the villages and into farmhouses adjoining their own enclosed land. Those who did not prosper under the new system gave up farming, and moved away to the towns and cities, taking up industrial jobs.

25.2 The Industrial Revolution

New technology and ideas also brought new techniques to Britain's traditional industries. This Industrial Revolution was to transform the working practices of the country and increase Britain's wealth substantially.

Iron

- Traditionally, iron was made by smelting – the process of heating iron ore and limestone together by burning charcoal. This produced pig iron, which was easy to work with, but not very strong. It could be melted into moulds to form cast iron, which was stronger but could be brittle.
- The trouble with this process was that charcoal was difficult and expensive to produce. Coal was an alternative, but it contained sulphur, which weakened the iron.
- In 1707, Abraham Darby discovered that the sulphur could be removed from coal by burning it in a confined space to produce 'coke'. As a cheaper and more plentiful alternative to charcoal, coke was very successful.
- Darby established an ironworks in Coalbrookdale in Shropshire, where, despite being a pacifist, he produced iron weapons and ammunition for the war against France.
- Darby's son, Abraham Darby II, heard of a primitive steam engine in nearby Dudley that could be used to work the bellows in the furnaces – a system much more efficient than their existing pumps, which were powered by a waterwheel.
- Cast iron was strong, but too brittle to be worked by hand. In 1784, Henry Cort patented a method of producing wrought iron from pig iron by 'puddling' – heating the iron with coal in a separate chamber, to prevent contamination with sulphur. This method took off and wrought iron became more popular than cast iron because it was far easier to work with.

- The cause was taken up by William Wilberforce, the MP for Hull, who raised questions on the issue in Parliament. Olaudah Equiano, an ex-slave who had written a book on his experiences, toured the country giving readings. Another supporter was the ceramics maker Josiah Wedgwood, who printed anti-slavery designs on his pots.
- The pro-slavery camp argued that losing the slave trade would allow other countries to take over Britain's colonies and achieve greater wealth, and that people had a better life as slaves than they did in Africa. Horatio Nelson declared himself a supporter.
- The anti-slavery campaigners succeeded in getting the Dolben Act passed through Parliament in 1788. This prevented too many slaves from being carried on a ship and forced ships to carry a surgeon to attend to their needs.
- Wilberforce tried but failed to pass anti-slavery Bills through Parliament in 1789 and 1791. The following year, Clarkson produced a book summarising the evidence he had presented to Parliament, which sold well and provoked hundreds of petitions.
- Parliament took steps to introduce laws against slavery, but the war against France intervened in 1793 and they were diverted on to other issues.

The gradual victory

- James Stephen, an anti-slavery lawyer resident in the West Indies, drew up a Bill that Wilberforce put through Parliament in 1806. It banned British ships and sailors from trading slaves with French colonies or allies of France. This seemed reasonable while Britain was fighting the French, and it made the slave trade much less profitable.
- This success encouraged others to take up the cause and the number of anti-slavery MPs in Parliament grew. Finally, in March 1807, a Bill banning the British slave trade passed through Parliament.
- Slavery was not yet completely abolished. New slaves could not be bought, but there were still thousands working on plantations across Britain's colonies. Their owners started to treat them better so that they were able to work for longer.
- The campaigners called for immediate abolition. They publicised the story of a young white missionary named John Smith, who had died in prison after encouraging a group of slaves in Guyana to revolt against their owners.

The final victory

- The Great Reform Act of 1832 meant that many anti-slavery MPs lost their seats in Parliament and the cause was weakened.
- Meanwhile, the slaves in the West Indies had heard about the steps being taken in Britain and they were getting restless. As more revolts broke out the government became concerned about a full-scale rebellion against British rule.
- A compromise was reached in Parliament in 1833. It was suggested that only slave children under six years old would be freed immediately – the rest would have to work as apprentices for their masters before being freed. The owners would also be compensated for losing their slaves.

- The Emancipation Act was passed in 1834, but the anti-slavery campaigners were angered by the compromises. It took another four years for the whole system to be dismantled and for slavery in Britain's colonies to end completely.

27.3 Prison reform

- As the Industrial Revolution encouraged more people to move into the towns and cities, the urban amenities, including prisons, were overwhelmed. Disease took hold amid the disgusting conditions, and prisoners had no opportunities for their own space or for exercise.
- Elizabeth Fry was a Quaker who visited prisons to attend to the poor. She became increasingly alarmed by the worsening conditions, and gathered a band of helpers who supplied new clothes and clean bedding.
- Fry organised a Ladies' Committee to visit the women prisoners every day. A school for the prisoners' children was started and the prisoners were encouraged to sew or knit, and to sell their products.
- Her advice was sought by the government for the reform of all prisons. As a Quaker she got rid of 'unhealthy' practices such as gambling, drinking and reading novels, which some resented. Others suggested that she was making prisoners too comfortable and that they were not getting the punishment they deserved.
- The British reforms spread over Europe and soon ladies' committees had been formed in France, and what are now Belgium and Germany.

27.4 Poor Law reform

- In the early nineteenth century the Poor Laws were over 200 years old. The Poor Rate was paid by villagers to be given to the poor in their own parish, but the rate varied.
- Now the Industrial Revolution had made the old system obsolete, as many had moved into the towns and cities, away from their home parish, and were allowed no relief.
- The Poor Law Commission was set up in 1832. It divided the poor into 'deserving' and 'undeserving' categories, and worked out the terms of the Act that was passed two years later.

The 1834 Poor Act

- Outdoor relief was discouraged. Relief was only offered if the poor were willing to live in a workhouse.
- Parishes were grouped into 'unions' and shared a workhouse between them.
- The rate of relief was standardised across the country.
- The workhouses were deliberately made uncomfortable so that people would be encouraged to leave and seek work themselves.

27.5 Employment reform

- The Industrial Revolution had caused many more of Britain's workforce to be employed by factories. There was very little regard given to the effect that these workplaces had on the health of the employees.

- Children were employed in cotton mills because they were small enough to move under the machinery to sweep up the small pieces of cloth. This was a dangerous environment and the children could easily be killed or maimed by the machines. There were no restrictions on their working hours.
- Some people began to notice the poor conditions, particularly in mines and cotton mills, and began to press for reform. A leading voice was Anthony Ashley Cooper, the seventh Earl of Shaftesbury, who spoke in Parliament on the need for better conditions.
- Some mill owners believed that employees worked better if they were treated well. A Scottish mill owner named Robert Owen regulated the working hours for his workers, and provided education and housing, but not many others followed his example.
- The Ten Hours Movement, set up in 1830, pressed for the working hours of children to be reduced to ten a day. They lost supporters in Parliament after the Great Reform Act of 1832. But Cooper attempted to pass a Bill through Parliament the following year, supported by a commission that had examined conditions in the cotton industry.
- The Bill failed to pass and the government pushed through their own legislation which became the Factory Act.

The Factory Act 1833

- Children under the age of nine were not allowed to work in factories.
- Children under the age of thirteen could not work more than nine hours a day.
- Children under the age of eighteen could not work more than twelve hours a day.
- Children under the age of eighteen were not allowed to work at night.
- All children had to be given two hours of education every day.

Further Factory Acts

- The reformers were very disappointed by the terms of the 1833 Act. The mill owners wanted children to work longer and they were often supported by the child's parents, who needed the extra income. It was also difficult to prove a child's age if the parents were not truthful.
- Parliament did not want to interfere with the relationship between employers and employees. Nonetheless, Cooper continued to press for further reform and succeeded in getting three more Factory Acts passed.
- The Factory Act 1844 banned women from working more than twelve hours a day, and those under thirteen from more than six and a half hours.
- The Factory Act 1847 banned both women and children from working more than ten hours.
- The Factory Act 1850 set the daily working hours for women and children as between 6am and 6pm, and required an hour's break for meals.
- In 1888 the women and girls working at the Bryant and May match factory in London went on strike, protesting against the long hours, poor pay and health risks of working with the dangerous phosphorous in the matches. Parliament forced the factory owners to improve conditions.
- London dockworkers went on strike the following year and also succeeded in improving their working conditions.

Revision tip

Use a flow chart with multiple strands to track the progress made by the abolitionists and reformers. The point of the chart is that you do not have to rewrite the whole narrative – just pick out the milestone events and the major figures involved in each struggle, and make use of abbreviations and pictures. For example, on the prison reform strand, start with the horrible conditions in the prisons before reform (disease and lack of space) and continue with Elizabeth Fry's efforts.

★ Make sure you know

- ★ The facts relating to the slave trade in the late eighteenth century.
- ★ The key events that led to the eventual abolition of slavery.
- ★ The key events surrounding the reform of prisons, led by Elizabeth Fry.
- ★ The key events surrounding the reform of the Poor Laws.
- ★ The key events surrounding the reform of employment conditions, led by Anthony Ashley Cooper.

Test yourself

Before moving on to the next chapter, make sure you can answer the following questions. The answers are at the back of the book.

1 Which Quaker was instrumental in first pressing for the abolition of slavery?

____

2 Which 1788 Act prevented too many slaves from being carried on a ship?

____

3 What was the name given to the groups founded by Elizabeth Fry that visited women's prisons?

____

4 Which Act of Parliament set the daily working hours for women and children as between 6am and 6pm?

____

Religious life, 1750–1914

28.1 Catholicism and the Oxford Movement

Attitudes towards Catholicism

In the years following the Glorious Revolution and the failed Jacobite Rebellions, Catholics were barely tolerated in England. By 1750, Catholics:

- Had limits placed on the property they could own.
- Had no right to vote.
- Had to pay special taxes.
- Could not join the armed forces.
- Could not educate their children as Catholics, whether at home or abroad.
- Could not occupy positions at the royal court or hold public office.

In 1778, desperate for more soldiers to fight in wars in America and France, the government passed the Papists Act. This allowed Catholics:

- To join the armed forces.
- To buy and inherit land.
- To form schools for Catholic education.
- In addition, rules against Catholic priests were relaxed.

In 1780 a group of Protestants, led by Lord George Gordon, drew up a petition demanding that the Papists Act be repealed.

- On 2 June, a crowd of up to 60,000 demonstrators marched to Parliament with the petition. They could not be controlled and a riot broke out by the House of Commons.
- Over the following week, the rioters rampaged through London, destroying public buildings and houses owned by prominent Catholics.
- On 7 June the army opened fire on the rioters. Nearly 300 people were killed and a further 200 wounded.

Large numbers of Catholic immigrants entered the United Kingdom.

- Many came to England to escape the violence of the French Revolution from 1789 onwards.
- When Ireland became part of the United Kingdom in 1801, its population of Catholics now had to be taken into account.

Pressure grew on Parliament to relax the anti-Catholic laws, and the Catholic Relief Act was passed in 1829. Catholics were now allowed to vote and could hold public office. In 1850 Catholic bishops were reintroduced to the United Kingdom.

The Oxford Movement

This movement, closely associated with men from the University of Oxford, argued for the English Church to return to old Catholic traditions.

- The men were known as Tractarians because they wrote and published 'tracts' which set out their views.
- Tractarians believed that there were three branches of a universal Catholic Church: Roman Catholicism, Anglicanism and Orthodoxy. They argued that elements of all three branches were compatible with each other.
- They reintroduced Roman Catholic symbolism and ceremony into their churches, such as the wearing of vestments, and use of candles and imagery.
- Notable Tractarians were John Henry Newman, Edward Bouverie Pusey and John Keble.

The Oxford Movement became highly influential, with many supporters, but also attracted criticism.

- Protestants who disagreed with the 'branch theory' naturally resisted the use of Catholic rituals.
- They claimed that the Tractarians secretly wanted to reintroduce the Roman Catholic Church as the state religion.
- Many supporters of the Oxford Movement did eventually convert to Catholicism, including Newman himself, which Protestants claimed supported their suspicions.

John Henry Newman (1801–90)

- Newman was an Oxford academic and Anglican priest, who was originally strongly Protestant. However, he began to have doubts about this during the 1830s and came to regard Catholicism as truer to the teachings in the Bible.
- He began writing tracts in 1833 and was joined by several other churchmen and academics.
- By 1842 he had renounced his belief in the branch theory and founded an Anglican monastery at Littlemore, Oxford. He converted to Catholicism in 1845.
- Newman founded oratories in Birmingham and London, and was appointed a cardinal by Pope Leo XIII in 1879.

Essay question

Try this sample essay question for yourself. A suggested answer is given at the back of the book.

Q Explain the significance of the Oxford Movement. (30)

29 Victorian England: success, war and politics

29.1 Victoria's life

Queen Victoria, still Britain's longest-serving monarch today, had a reign that spanned a multitude of social, political and cultural changes.

- Victoria was the daughter of Edward, Duke of Kent, and Princess Victoria of Saxe-Coburg-Saalfeld. Her father died when she was a child and she fell increasingly under the control of her domineering mother.
- Victoria was the only surviving grandchild of King George III and, as such, was next in line to her uncle, William IV. When William died in June 1837, Victoria became Queen, aged just eighteen. She immediately moved away from her mother's influence.
- Victoria was known to be beautiful and intelligent, but also headstrong and stubborn. She hated dealing with people she disliked and only wanted to surround herself with friends.
- Victoria married her cousin, Prince Albert of Saxe-Coburg, in 1840. As a foreigner, Albert was viewed with suspicion in Britain but worked hard to gain people's trust. He managed the royal estates and helped to promote cultural attractions for the people.
- When Prince Albert died in 1861 Victoria was devastated and wore mourning clothes for the rest of her life. She shut herself away from the public but still handled affairs of state as efficiently as before.
- Victoria and Albert's children married into other European royal families and strengthened the political ties between Britain and Europe, particularly with Germany and Russia.
- Her Golden and Diamond Jubilees were celebrated in 1887 and 1897 with widespread celebrations throughout the Empire. Victoria died in January 1901, and the throne passed to her eldest son, who became King Edward VII.

29.2 Victorian politics

The Whig Prime Minister Lord Melbourne helped Victoria a great deal with her new position and defended her against those who felt she was unsuitably young. But in 1839 he lost an important debate in Parliament and resigned. The Tory leader Robert Peel was asked to take over but requested that Melbourne's friends in the royal household be replaced with his allies. In what became known as the Bedchamber Crisis, Victoria refused, claiming that her household was her business alone. She was forced to back down when Peel won a general election decisively in 1841.

The repeal of the Corn Laws

- Peel was particularly interested in the economy and promoted 'free trade' – the idea that people should be able to deal in goods across national borders without having to pay import or export taxes.

- Peel was also against changes to the established order, and opposed the 1832 Reform Act and the demands of the Chartists.
- The Corn Laws had been passed in 1815 to protect the price of corn after the Napoleonic wars. Peel argued that they stood against free trade and that they caused hardship by making the price of bread artificially high. He was not supported by fellow Tories who grew crops on their land.
- The Corn Laws were only repealed because the Whigs supported it; 222 Tories had opposed it and the issue split the party between 'Peelites' and 'Protectionists'.

Gladstone and Disraeli

- William Gladstone and Benjamin Disraeli were on opposite sides of the Tory split. Disraeli opposed Peel, while Gladstone supported him but was not in Parliament at the time.
- Gladstone remained loyal to Peel when his government collapsed, but later joined the Whigs in 1859 and formed a new party, the Liberals.
- Disraeli had a Jewish background and was a successful author before going to Parliament, both of which made him feel like something of an outsider. After the collapse of the Tories he became leader of the Conservative party that was formed to replace them.
- Gladstone led the Liberals to government in 1868 and passed a large number of Acts dealing in social reform. They passed the 1870 Elementary Education Act, which established compulsory free schools for children up to the age of eleven. Despite this, Gladstone did not generally feel very strongly about social reform and felt that the poor ought to help themselves.
- In 1886, during his third term in government, Gladstone decided to grant Ireland a small amount of independence, known as Home Rule, in order to control the increasing unrest there. This split the Liberal party and many Liberals joined the Conservatives, who strongly opposed the idea.
- Disraeli also passed reforming acts but valued the Conservative party above everything and would not do anything to provoke a damaging split. Two Factory Acts in 1874 and 1878 reduced working hours, and required working conditions to be inspected and approved by government officials.
- In 1875 Disraeli managed to buy a 44 per cent share in the Suez Canal, which was an important route to Asia, connecting Britain with the Empire. He created the title Empress of India for Queen Victoria and became her favourite politician.
- As the Ottoman Empire declined and Russia declared war on the Turks, Disraeli helped to broker a peace between the nations at the Congress of Berlin in 1878. Britain also gained the island of Cyprus from the Turks.

Test yourself

Before moving on to the next chapter, make sure you can answer the following questions. The answers are at the back of the book.

1 What was the name given to the crisis caused by Victoria's refusal to change her household staff?

____

2 Which 1870 Act established free schooling for children?

____

3 What was the name given to the building housing the Great Exhibition?

____

4 What was the name of the officer's centre set up near Sevastopol by Mary Seacole?

____

5 What was the nickname given to Florence Nightingale?

____

6 Which suffragette was killed attempting a protest at the Epsom Derby in 1913?

____

The British Empire and the road to war

30.1 India

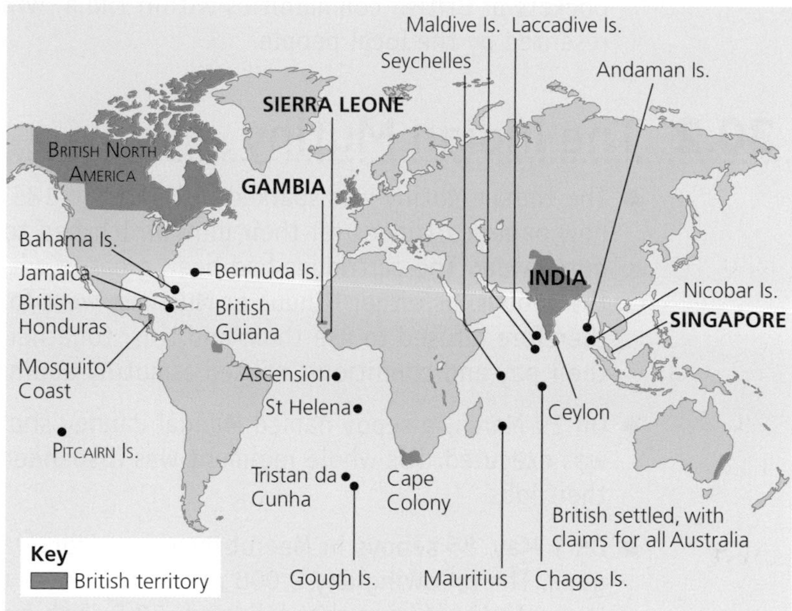

■ Map of the British Empire at the end of the Napoleonic Wars in 1815

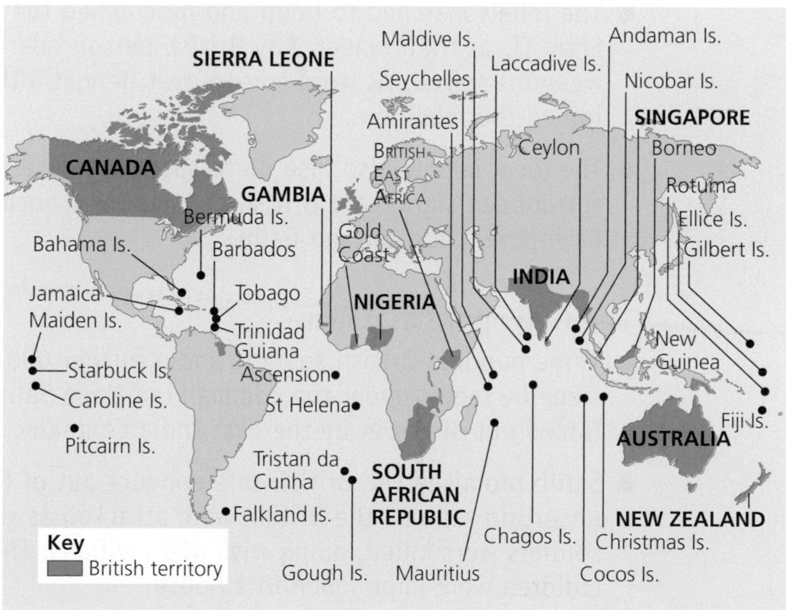

■ Map of the British Empire at the end of the nineteenth century

- Britain's interests in India were controlled by the East India Company, founded in 1600, with the trade mainly in goods such as tea, cotton, spices and silk. It worked with local rulers and grew to become the largest trading company in India, seeing off competition from other European powers.

- In 1757, Robert Clive won the Battle of Plassey against the Nawab of Bengal and his French supporters. The East India Company then took over the running of Bengal, collecting taxes and administering the justice systems.
- The East India Company hired local men, known as sepoys, to be trained as soldiers in the British fashion and to give military force to the company's rule.
- As British traders and officers began to settle in Bengal under the company's rule, they brought their wives and families. This caused small pockets of British communities within India, which were distrusted and resented by the local people.

30.2 The Indian Mutiny

- The Indian Mutiny was sparked in Meerut in 1857. The sepoys were given new paper cartridges for their guns which had to be bitten to release the gunpowder. The cartridges had been greased with cow or pig fat which the sepoys, as either Hindus or Muslims, were forbidden to touch. They therefore refused to use them and this, together with discontent about their pay and conditions, caused a mutiny against the British.
- On 29 March, a sepoy named Mangal Pandey shot at a British officer and was executed. His whole regiment was disbanded and the other sepoys lost their jobs.
- On 9 May, 85 sepoys in Meerut were imprisoned for refusing to use their guns. The following day 2,000 others took over the prison and freed them. In the rioting that followed, 50 British men and several women and children were killed.
- The rebels marched to Delhi and proclaimed the Mughal Emperor, Bahadur Shah II, as their leader. Any British person nearby was killed and their weapons seized. As word spread over Bengal, other sepoys mutinied and joined the rebellion.
- The local people also rose up to support the sepoys. Together the rebels surrounded significant British communities, including civilians, at Cawnpore, Lucknow and Delhi.

The Cawnpore massacre

- Three hundred British soldiers and a further 600 civilians were held under siege by rebels under the command of Nana Sahib, a prince who had been forced out of power by the East India Company.
- Sahib promised the British safe conduct out of Cawnpore by boat, but for uncertain reasons the British were attacked as they embarked. All 300 soldiers were killed, along with 400 civilians. The surviving 200 women and children were imprisoned in a house.
- On 15 July, Sahib and his men were defeated by General Henry Havelock. The following day the British discovered that the prisoners had been butchered where they were held, apparently on the orders of Sahib.
- The British were outraged by the massacre and sought their revenge on the sepoys, burning the surrounding villages and killing any sepoy who tried to surrender.

Lucknow

- The 800 British soldiers and 500 civilians in Lucknow were able to shelter in the fortified British Residency there, and initially had access to food and water. But supplies began to run out during August and September.
- General Havelock's troops were reinforced by those of Major-General Sir James Outram, and they were able to advance on Lucknow. They fought their way into the city on 25 September.
- On reaching the British Residency, Havelock and Outram found there were so many sick and wounded that they could not be moved. Instead Havelock joined the besieged people and sent a message asking for more reinforcements.
- The relief force, under the command of General Colin Campbell, fought its way into Lucknow on 17 November and evacuated the British at the Residency.
- The rebels in Lucknow held out until March 1858, when the city fell back into British hands completely.

Delhi

- As the capital of the Mughal Empire, Delhi was the most significant city to be held under siege. It was important for morale that the British should regain it.
- It took six days for the city to be retaken by the British, which was achieved on 19 September. Bahadur Shah II was captured trying to flee the city.
- The British lost 3,000 men in the battle for Delhi.
- Fighting continued into the following year. Those found guilty of inciting rebellion, or of participating in the massacres, were hanged or blown apart by cannons.

Consequences of the mutiny

- The government looked into the causes of the uprising and found the practices of the East India Company to be at fault.
- The structure of the army was modified to allow locals to achieve higher ranks and British officers were encouraged to mix with the locals.
- The local government in India was also reorganised to allow locals to rise to higher office.
- More respect was paid generally to Indian customs, and traditions that did not conflict with British rule were allowed to continue.
- Nonetheless, Britain was keen to re-establish its rule and discourage any further mutiny. Queen Victoria was given the title Empress of India, which emphasised just who was in charge.

30.3 South Africa

- South Africa was first taken by the British from the Dutch during the Napoleonic Wars. The Dutch settlers, or Boers, travelled north to establish their own states, the Transvaal and the Orange Free State.
- When diamonds were found on a remote farm in 1871, thousands of people flocked there and established the town of Kimberley. The British annexed the Transvaal in 1877 and defeated the Zulus, who also wanted to regain the land from the Boers.
- Three years later, the Transvaal declared its independence and Britain went to war with the Boers, but eventually agreed peace terms.
- An Englishman, Cecil Rhodes, had controlled the de Beers mining company in Kimberley and now became Governor of Cape Colony. He started mining for gold in the Transvaal, and annexed two areas for mining that became known as Northern and Southern Rhodesia.
- The town of Johannesburg was established at the spot where gold was found in the Transvaal. This led to thousands of Uitlanders – or outsiders – coming into the country. Paul Kruger, President of the Transvaal, did not want to give these settlers the vote, which allowed the British to argue that they were being treated unfairly.
- In 1896 Rhodes organised a raid into the Transvaal to provoke the Uitlanders into rebellion. The plot was discovered and Rhodes had to give up his position.
- Sir Alfred Milner, the British High Commissioner, believed that the Boers needed to be pushed out of both the Transvaal and Cape Colony by force. In the meantime, the Boers armed themselves with weapons bought from Germany.
- By October 1899, three groups were ready for war: the British, who had sent 10,000 soldiers to South Africa; the Boers, who had greater experience of fighting in the veld grasslands of South Africa; and the black Africans, who were used as labourers and servants by both sides.

30.4 The Anglo-Boer War, 1899–1902

The Boer War can be divided into three stages:

- The Boer offensives
- The British offensives
- Guerrilla war and stalemate

The Boer offensives

- The Boers acted swiftly and surrounded large British forces at Ladysmith, Mafeking and Kimberley.
- General Sir Redvers Buller sent Lord Methuen to relieve Kimberley and Mafeking, and set out for Ladysmith himself, before planning to march into the Transvaal and Orange Free State.
- The Boers set a trap for Lord Methuen's men at Magersfontein by concealing themselves in hidden trenches and opening fire suddenly – 950 British soldiers were killed.

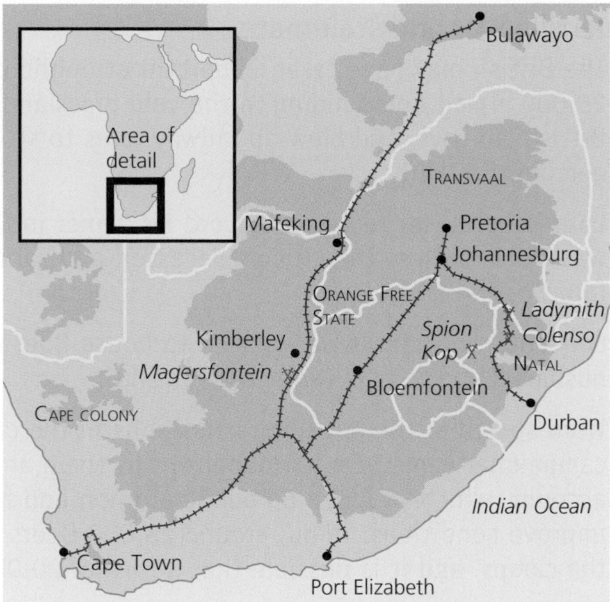

■ A map showing where the Boer attacked at the beginning of the war and the early battles of Magersfontein, Colenso and Spion Kop

- Buller's men were also defeated when trying to cross the Tugela River at Colenso. He turned his efforts elsewhere and, together with General Warren, tried to break through the Boer defences surrounding Ladysmith by sending British troops over a hill named Spion Kop.
- The British succeeded in taking the hill on 3 January 1900, but found themselves surrounded by Boers on neighbouring hills, who bombarded them with artillery fire.
- The British retreated from Spion Kop, but managed to take some nearby high ground named Twin Peaks. The Boers struggled to keep up but inflicted heavy losses on the British – 1,500 men were lost in all.

The British offensives

- Buller was replaced by Lord Roberts, who brought with him an army that was better equipped, with cavalry units. He decided not to attack the Boers head on, but to surround them with British horsemen.
- The new tactic worked at Kimberley, where the siege was lifted on 15 February 1900.
- The Boers, under General Cronje, fled northwards but became trapped at Paardeberg, where they were surrounded by British cavalry. Cronje withstood two weeks of bombardment but surrendered on 27 February.
- The following day, Buller managed to cross the Tugela River and relieved the siege at Ladysmith. Bloemfontein, the capital of the Orange Free State, also fell to the British.
- Mafeking was relieved on 17 May, and was held up as an example of British courage and resolve. The British commander there, Colonel Robert Baden-Powell, had withstood the siege with only a small force for 217 days.
- Lord Roberts marched into Pretoria, the capital of the Transvaal, on 5 June and President Kruger fled.

Guerrilla war and stalemate

- The British may have taken important strongholds but there were still 25,000 armed Boers hiding in the veld grasslands. These men led raids on British convoys, and blew up railway lines to stop supplies and troops from getting through.
- Lord Roberts was replaced by Lord Kitchener in December 1900. Kitchener was more ruthless than his predecessor, and sanctioned the burning of Boer farms and villages.
- Concentration camps were set up to house Boer women and children whose husbands and fathers were still fighting.
- Word spread of the appalling conditions in the camps. An anti-war campaigner named Emily Hobhouse saw them and wrote a damning account, which whipped up public opinion and forced the government to improve conditions. In all, around 28,000 Boers, mostly children, died in the camps, and it is possible that a further 20,000 black Africans died, too.
- Slowly the Boer commandos in the field began to run out of supplies. The British showed no signs of giving up and eventually even the Boer generals were calling for peace.
- In May 1902, the remaining Boer fighters agreed to surrender.

Consequences of the Boer War

- The British had lost close to 100,000 men during the Boer campaign. The Boers lost around 7,000 soldiers and 28,000 civilians.
- The Transvaal and Orange Free State were taken and rebuilt by the British and, along with the Cape Colony, formed into the Union of South Africa in 1910.
- The British had found that their army was not as effective fighting a large campaign, having grown used to small colonial conflicts in the past. Lessons were learned and reforms made to make the military more efficient.
- Britain had also relied heavily on its Empire to fight the war, as no help was forthcoming from other strong powers such as Russia or France. This encouraged Britain to create alliances with these countries to make its military position stronger for the future.

Revision tip

You will need to recall the timelines of the Indian Mutiny and the Anglo-Boer War. Draw each one as a flowchart in chronological order and include what sparked the conflict (new cartridges for the sepoys in India), the crucial battles fought and their outcomes (for example Magersfontein and Spion Kop), and the consequences of British victory.

Essay question

Try this sample essay question for yourself. A suggested answer is given at the back of the book.

Q Explain the most important consequences of the Anglo-Boer War of 1899–1902. (30)

30.5 Great Power rivalries, 1871–1914

The Great Powers of Europe during this period were Britain, France, Germany, Italy, Austria-Hungary and Russia.

The Franco-Prussian War (1870–71)

- Germany (which then consisted of several independent states) invaded France in 1870. Germany won and became a single unified country that was able to dominate Europe.
- France was left in chaos, and lost the two eastern provinces of Alsace and Lorraine to Germany. For years the French resented this and wanted revenge on Germany.

The alliances

- Dual Alliance (1879) – Germany allied with Austria-Hungary. Italy joined and formed the Triple Alliance (1882).
- Franco-Russian Alliance (1894).
- Entente Cordiale (1904) – Britain allied with France. Russia joined and formed the Triple Entente (1907).
- By 1907, Europe was divided into two opposing blocs: Britain, France and Russia (the Allied Powers) on one side, and Germany, Austria-Hungary and Italy (the Central Powers) on the other.

Colonisation and the scramble for Africa

- By 1880 Britain and France had the largest empires in the world. The other Great Powers saw an opportunity to gain wealth by doing the same. They looked particularly to Africa as a land that was rich in resources and relatively easy to take over by force.
- In 1881 Britain invaded Egypt and France took over Tunisia. This sparked the 'scramble for Africa' as other countries raced to gain as many colonies as they could.
- Belgium took the Congo, Italy took Eritrea, and Germany took Togoland, Cameroon and South-West Africa. France took land in West Africa.
- By 1914 virtually all of Africa (except Ethiopia) had been colonised by the Great Powers. Britain held the most, followed by France and Germany.

The arms race

- In addition to the scramble for Africa, the Great Powers built up their armed forces substantially after 1880.
- Some countries introduced conscription, with a standing army (ready at all times) and 'reservists', who undertook training over the summer and were on standby for up to twenty years.
- By 1900 Germany had 500,000 soldiers in a standing army and a further 3.4 million reservists.
- Between 1898 and 1912 Germany expanded its navy considerably. Britain, who had by far the largest navy, also expanded in response. By 1914 Britain had still managed to keep its navy around twice the size of Germany's.

★ Make sure you know

- ★ The background to British rule in India.
- ★ The key causes, events and consequences of the Indian Mutiny of 1857.
- ★ The background to British rule in South Africa.
- ★ The key causes, events and consequences of the Anglo-Boer War of 1899–1902.
- ★ The key facts surrounding the Great Power rivalries between 1871 and 1914.

Test yourself ✓

Before moving on to the next chapter, make sure you can answer the following questions. The answers are at the back of the book.

1 Which British military leader won the Battle of Plassey in 1757?

____

2 Who was the Mughal Emperor at the time of the Indian Mutiny?

____

3 By what term did the Boers refer to outsiders living in the Transvaal?

____

4 At which siege did General Cronje surrender his Boer soldiers in 1900?

____

5 Which 1904 alliance was agreed between Britain and France?

____

Essay question answers

These suggested answers to the sample essay questions are intended to provide pointers to the way you structure your answers in the exam. Check your answers against these points. You will be expected to write your answers in **full prose** and marks may be awarded for the quality of your writing. Be aware that an answer which simply lists these points with no attempt to evaluate and show judgement will only achieve a 50 per cent mark at best. Your best approach is to create an argument, perhaps that one factor is more important than another, or examine two sides of the question. For example, look at the following essay question on William I. One approach to this essay is to look at the different approaches used by William to control England and argue how one was more successful or had a greater impact than the others.

Chapter 2

Explain how William I dealt with opposition to his rule. (30)

- The English earls Edwin and Morcar rebelled against William in 1069.
- They were aided in their rebellion by some Vikings and Scots.
- The Norman soldiers stationed at York were killed.
- In response, William ordered his soldiers to lay waste to large areas of Yorkshire. The people were killed, their homes looted and land burned.
- This has become known as the 'Harrying of the North'.
- William introduced the Feudal System to England. This was a series of agreements of loyalty, which ran from the King down to the peasants.
- The nobles under the King were obliged to provide a number of men for military service.
- The Feudal System assured William of his nobles' loyalty and guaranteed that they could gather him an army.
- The 'Harrying of the North' in 1069 was a brutal method of control – it effectively wiped out large areas of resistance.
- The Normans also introduced new castles to England. These were motte and baileys that could be built quickly and cheaply.
- Positions of authority, such as earls and bishops, were filled by Normans.
- By compiling the Domesday Book, William was able to find out exactly how many soldiers he could hope to gather for an army.

Chapter 3

Explain the significance of the Church on life in England in the Middle Ages. (30)

- Bishops were significant landholders and could raise Church taxes called tithes.
- Monasteries provided education for youngsters who joined the order. Monasteries had large libraries full of books, which the monks would make copies of.
- Monasteries gave food to the poor and shelter to travellers. Often, local people would be employed as servants.

- The village priest would baptise babies, marry couples and bury the dead.
- Priests preached that those who did not follow their religion would go to Hell. The people were reminded of Hell by murals painted on church walls.
- Mass was spoken in Latin, which only the educated could understand.
- Local people gave gifts of money to monasteries because they believed that this would secure them a place in Heaven.

Chapter 8

Explain the significance of the Peasants' Revolt. (30)

- The government introduced a Poll Tax in 1377. This was repeated in 1379 and again in 1381.
- By 1381, the Poll Tax had been raised to one shilling, which most peasants could not hope to afford. This was especially the case with villeins, who were not paid for working on the land.
- The peasants took out their frustrations on the tax collectors. Soon the discontent spread to the counties surrounding London in the south-east and some government agents were killed.
- The rebels were encouraged to march by leaders such as Wat Tyler from Kent.
- The peasants marched on London mostly because of high tax rises. But they had been demanding to be paid for some years and were now beginning to question why people in authority had more rights than they had. Some no longer wanted to support the war in France or the authority of the Church.
- The Peasants' Revolt was a significant uprising from a monarch's ordinary subjects.
- Richard II was able to gain control through his assurances to the rebels. But he did not keep his promises, and trust in him was lost.
- Richard's victory caused him to become over-confident and he tried to force Parliament into granting him more control. This eventually led to his downfall in 1399 and the accession of Henry IV.

Chapter 9

Explain the importance of the life of Joan of Arc. (30)

- Joan of Arc believed that as a young girl she received messages from God. She wished to throw the English out of France.
- She was supported by the Dauphin, who asked her to save the city of Orléans.
- Joan was able to break the siege and free Orléans, and helped other cities held by the English, including Reims.
- Joan was unable to free Paris and was captured by the English. She was accused of witchcraft, tried and executed.
- Joan's actions strengthened the perception of Henry VI being a weak king and caused him large losses in France, which caused resentment among his nobles.
- Joan was a popular leader thanks to her ability in commanding an army, and had a number of successes.

- She was also popular with the French people because of her youth, devotion to God and the fact that she was female. After her death the story of her life and achievements was retold, causing it to become legendary.

Chapter 11

Explain how Henry VII dealt with opposition to his rule. (30)

- Henry VII replaced Yorkist nobles with those who had supported him. Lancastrian nobles who had had their lands taken by Edward IV now had them restored.
- The Court of Star Chamber was set up to deal with any rebellion provoked by the nobility. The court could confiscate land and issue fines.
- Justices of the Peace were appointed all over the country to keep order and promote the courts outside of London.
- The Law of Livery restricted nobles from retaining a large private army. They also had to sign a recognisance by which they agreed to give up a sum of money if they were disloyal.
- The influence of the nobility was removed from the government as Henry appointed lesser members of the gentry to his Council and to run the court system.
- The Council of Wales and Council of the North were formed to take care of areas where the nobles were not as supportive of Henry.
- Henry needed to control his nobles because he recognised that a strong nobility would pose more of a threat if it turned against him.
- Loyal nobles were encouraged to stay loyal by the threat of severe punishment if they rebelled. The most loyal were rewarded with gifts of land that had been taken from Yorkists.
- The removal of nobles from Henry's Council meant that he could now rely on the advice of educated men in dealing with threats to his rule.
- The courts' use of fines raised a lot of money for the royal treasury – sufficient for the King to raise a strong army if he needed to.
- The Council of Wales and Council of the North, as well as the appointment of Justices of the Peace, meant that the King had some sort of royal presence everywhere in the country.

Chapter 15

Explain how the process of enclosure led to unrest in the countryside. (30)

- Enclosure was a process that allowed a change in land use from arable farming to pastoral farming.
- First, the open fields were divided into separate areas. Second, the common land of each manor was fenced off.
- In medieval times each manor had open fields, upon which the peasants each farmed a strip. Enclosure meant that the lords divided the whole field into smaller fields for grazing animals.
- The area of common land in each manor used to be available for all the people to graze whatever animals they had. Enclosure meant that the lords took these for themselves and used them to graze their own livestock.

- The process of enclosure was characterised by the erection of permanent fences and walls, either to divide up the large open fields or to fence off the old common land from the people.
- The enclosure movement led to unrest in the countryside because the peasants found themselves either without jobs or without land to farm themselves.
- Some peasants relied on renting land from their lords, to produce their own crops to eat, sell or feed to their animals. This land was taken away and the peasants were left without access to food.
- Pastoral farming was not as labour intensive, meaning that fewer men were needed to do the work. The peasants who worked their lords' land for pay, found themselves without a source of income.
- The loss of the common land meant that any peasants who owned animals no longer had any land on which to graze them. The animals could not exercise or grow effectively, and another source of food and income was lost.
- The discontent over enclosure led to uprisings such as Kett's Rebellion in 1549.

Chapter 17

Explain why there might have been opposition to the ceremony appointing Oliver Cromwell as Lord Protector in 1657. (30)

- When Oliver Cromwell was appointed Lord Protector he intended to rule closely with Parliament. However, he decided to call in the army instead when certain MPs threatened to support the restoration of the monarchy.
- Cromwell introduced laws that made people's way of life as Puritan as possible. Any form of 'Catholic' festival or ceremony was banned.
- Cromwell's appointment as Lord Protector was not formalised until 1657, after he discussed a new English constitution with his army leaders.
- The army leaders did not want Cromwell to be sworn in to his position in the same manner as a king.
- There was a strong opinion that Cromwell should not be seen as a replacement for Charles I, whom they had fought so hard to get rid of. The army believed that, once Cromwell was dead, this might encourage Charles' son to continue his efforts to reclaim the throne.
- Cromwell had outlawed Catholicism and made church services conform to extreme Protestantism in terms of imagery and mode of dress, which were modest.
- Any opposition to the ceremony in 1657 would have been because it was very similar to a king's coronation. It was a magnificent occasion with much wealth on display, which many would have believed to have gone against Cromwell's Puritan principles.

Chapter 20

Explain why the 1745 Jacobite Rebellion was not successful. (30)

- Charles Edward Stuart, in exile in France, sailed to Scotland and landed on the island of Eriskay in July 1745. He marched across the Highlands, gathering support as he went.
- Charles' army defeated a government army at the Battle of Prestonpans in September 1745. They then marched south, across the border and into England.
- The Jacobites reached Derby, but were persuaded to turn back due to lack of support. They received reinforcements in Scotland and won another battle against a government army at Falkirk in January 1746.
- A new government army, led by William, Duke of Cumberland, marched north and met the Jacobites on Culloden Moor on 16 April 1746.
- During the battle that followed, the well-trained government soldiers were able to defeat the undisciplined Highlanders. The Jacobites scattered all over Scotland and Charles fled back to France.
- The 1745 Jacobite Rebellion was not successful because of the inability of the Jacobites to gain widespread support, Charles Edward Stuart's inexperience in battle and the superiority of the government army under the Duke of Cumberland.
- When Charles first marched through Scotland he was able to gain the support of several Scottish clans. But many others remained loyal and some even fought on the government side at Culloden.
- The Jacobites were unable to gain further support during the march south through England. There may have been sympathetic English Catholics who were simply unwilling to accept him as King.
- Charles was inexperienced but stubborn. He refused to listen to his generals at Culloden, who advised him to avoid battle until they found a location more suited to them. His successes at Prestonpans and Falkirk had made him over-confident.
- The government army at Culloden was far superior in its tactics, discipline and fighting skills. While the Highlanders charged in a disorganised manner, the government soldiers were well trained and held their positions.

Chapter 21

Explain the importance of the role of James Wolfe in the Battle of the Plains of Abraham. (30)

- Major-General James Wolfe had served in the army for nearly twenty years. He was popular with his men, but was viewed with suspicion by his peers.
- Prime Minister Pitt instructed Wolfe to take the city of Quebec, which was built at the top of a steep cliff and defended by General Montcalm with 16,000 men.
- Wolfe had fewer than 10,000 men but was supported by a huge navy. These ships sailed up the St Lawrence River in June 1759 and set their guns on Quebec.

- On the night of 12 September, Wolfe led a small band of men up the cliff side, overpowering the French militia at the top. The path was cleared for the rest of Wolfe's army to follow.
- The Battle of the Plains of Abraham was fought the next day. Both commanders, Wolfe and Montcalm, were killed, along with 58 British and 500 French troops.
- The French were routed and forced back into the city of Quebec, which fell to the British five days later.
- The assault on the cliffs was a daring operation that carried a large risk. But Wolfe's boldness, and the respect he had earned from his men, allowed it to be successful.
- Wolfe led from the front and commanded his men from the centre of the fighting. This was an effective strategy that led to victory, but also to his own death.

Chapter 23

Explain whether William Pitt the Younger was successful as Prime Minister. (30)

- William Pitt became Prime Minister aged just 24.
- He reformed the tax system, clamped down on smuggling and removed corrupt government officials.
- Pitt's government instead gave support to the loyalists, who opposed the radicals that called for revolution.
- He suspended the right of *habeas corpus*, and the government outlawed large public meetings and trade unions.
- Pitt also persuaded other countries to fight by promising money and arms if they declared war on France.
- His military tactic was to use the British navy to blockade the French in their own ports, and to seize the French colonies so that Britain could grow wealthier from an expanded empire.
- Pitt served as Prime Minister for seventeen years. He had an extremely high ability and maturity, suggested by his being Britain's youngest ever Prime Minister.
- His domestic policies helped to improve Britain's economy after the American War of Independence.
- Fearing a revolution similar to the one in France, he was also successful in keeping the radicals in check.
- His military tactics, however, could not prevent France from building alliances with other countries and drawing Britain into a land war.

Chapter 24

Explain the significance of the 1832 Great Reform Bill. (30)

- Before the Great Reform Bill, Britain's political system was unbalanced and unrepresentative. Members of Parliament could represent thousands of voters, or as few as 40.
- There was no secret ballot and voting was done openly. This meant that voters could be coerced into voting a particular way.
- After the Great Reform Bill, the electorate probably increased from 500,000 to 813,000.
- One out of every seven men could now vote. The worst 'rotten boroughs' were abolished and their electorate taken up by larger towns.
- The political party system began to take shape in order to attract new voters.
- The Crown's control over the political system began to decrease as Parliament no longer needed as much royal approval.
- The Bill did not, however, iron out all the unfairness of the old system.
- The population of Britain was 24 million people, so still only a very small minority could vote.
- The voters were still wealthy men and there was still no secret ballot.
- MPs were unpaid and so needed plenty of private money and spare time to serve in Parliament. So it took some time for middle-class MPs to be elected, although middle-class politicians became more active in local government.

Chapter 28

Explain the significance of the Oxford Movement. (30)

- The Oxford Movement consisted of men who were known as Tractarians because they wrote and published 'tracts'.
- Tractarians believed that there were three branches of a universal Catholic church: Roman Catholicism, Anglicanism, and Orthodoxy. They argued that elements of all three branches were compatible with each other.
- They reintroduced Roman Catholic symbolism and ceremony into their churches, such as the wearing of vestments and use of candles and imagery.
- Protestants who disagreed with the 'branch theory' naturally resisted the use of Catholic rituals. They claimed that the Tractarians secretly wanted to reintroduce the Roman Catholic church as the state religion.
- Many supporters of the Oxford Movement did eventually convert to Catholicism, including John Henry Newman, which Protestants claimed supported their suspicions.
- Tractarians were successful in moving the Church of England away from exclusively 'Protestant' styles of worship.
- The Oxford Movement coincided with the emancipation of Catholics and they took advantage of this to develop their beliefs.
- Today, Anglican worship encompasses many different styles, and the worshipper has the choice of which style they would like to follow.

Chapter 30

Explain the most important consequences of the Anglo-Boer War of 1899–1902. (30)

- The British lost nearly 100,000 men during the Boer campaign. The Boers lost around 7,000 soldiers and 28,000 civilians.
- The Transvaal and Orange Free State were taken and rebuilt by the British, who reintroduced their system of government.
- The Union of South Africa, which included the Cape Colony, was formed by the British in 1910.
- The British had found that their army was not as effective in fighting a large campaign, having grown used to small colonial conflicts in the past. The British armed forces were reformed to make them more efficient.
- Britain had also relied heavily on its Empire to fight the war, as no help was forthcoming from other strong powers, such as Russia or France.
- This encouraged Britain to create alliances with these countries to make its military position stronger for the future.
- This, in turn, was a major cause of the events which led to the First World War.

Test yourself answers

Chapter 1

1 William claimed Harold swore an oath that he would support William's claim to the English throne.

2 Tostig Godwinson supported Harald Hardrada.

3 The Witan was a council that included the most important nobles and churchmen in England.

4 The Normans landed at Pevensey on 28 September 1066.

5 The battle between Harold and William was fought at Senlac Hill, near Hastings, on 14 October 1066.

Chapter 2

1 A landholder who swore fealty became a vassal to his lord.

2 Edwin and Morcar reclaimed York from the Normans in 1069.

3 The typical features of Norman churches were thick stone walls, and rounded arches over the doors and windows.

4 The Domesday Book refers to the time in the reign of King Edward, when the land was granted by William and at the time of the survey.

5 Cottars were paid wages to work.

6 The land belonging to the lord of the manor was known as his demesne.

Chapter 3

1 Archbishop Anselm of Canterbury quarrelled with William II.

2 Henry I had one surviving legitimate child, a daughter. He wanted her to take over the throne after him, but many nobles did not like the idea of a woman leading the country.

3 Murals were painted on church walls to give a religious message to those who could not read. The murals often depicted Hell, as a reminder of what awaited them if they sinned.

4 If a monastery became wealthy, the monks might allow themselves more luxuries. Therefore the rules of St Benedict – which urged a simple life with no possessions – would not be followed.

Chapter 4

1 The three points of the Constitutions of Clarendon that Thomas Becket refused to accept were those that stated no one could be excommunicated without the King's permission; no churchman could leave England without the King's permission; and criminous clerks would be sentenced by the royal courts.

2 The Pope objected when Henry II tried to use Archbishop Roger of York for the coronation of his son.

3 Henry II's sons Henry, Richard and Geoffrey, and their mother Eleanor of Aquitaine, were all involved in the 1173 revolt against the King.

Chapter 5

1 The crusaders captured Antioch in 1098.

2 The terms of the 1192 truce stated that Richard could keep all the land he had conquered down to Jaffa, but everything south of the city, including Jerusalem, had to be left for Saladin.

3 Pope Innocent III placed England under an interdict in 1208.

4 The Magna Carta was presented to John at Runnymede, near Windsor, in 1215.

Chapter 6

1 Simon de Montfort was killed at the Battle of Evesham in 1265.

2 Edward I twice defeated Llewelyn of Wales by cutting off the Welsh supply line from Anglesey.

3 A Scottish rebel army led by William Wallace won the Battle of Stirling Bridge in 1297.

4 The English retreated quickly from the battlefield at Bannockburn because they thought that the Scots were receiving reinforcements. In fact, these were just ordinary people and not soldiers.

5 Roger Mortimer plotted with Isabella of France to overthrow Edward II.

Chapter 7

1 Edward I's castles in Wales were made up of concentric rings.

2 An anti-Jewish attack is called a pogrom.

3 Margaret Paston handled her husband's business during his absence.

4 *Yersinia pestis* is the bacteria that causes bubonic plague.

5 Flagellants were people who believed that by whipping themselves they would pay penance for other people's sins and therefore stop the Plague, which they saw as a punishment from God.

Chapter 8

1 The Poll Tax was raised in 1377, 1379 and 1381.

2 In 1397, Richard II dealt with the Lords Appellant by having one executed, another murdered and the other three sent into exile.

3 An apprentice was held in the service of a master craftsman by an agreement called an indenture.

4 A charter was needed for a town to appoint its own government.

Chapter 9

1 Owain Glyndwr fought at the Battle of Shrewsbury in 1403.

2 A swift attack with horses for pillage was called a *chevauchée*.

3 Joan of Arc was convicted of being a witch, allowing the English to execute her.

4 Jack Cade led the Kentish rebellion of 1450.

Chapter 10

1 The symbols of the Yorkists and the Lancastrians were the white rose and the red rose, respectively.

2 Richard Neville, Earl of Warwick, is often known as the 'Kingmaker'.

3 Prince Edward was killed at the Battle of Tewkesbury in 1471.

4 Richard III claimed that the marriage between Edward IV and Elizabeth Woodville had been invalid. Therefore any children they had would have been illegitimate and, thus, Edward V would have been barred from the throne.

5 The Earl of Northumberland failed to come to the aid of Richard III at the Battle of Bosworth.

Chapter 11

1 Holding a personal army was called retaining.

2 Perkin Warbeck claimed to be Richard of York, the younger of the two 'Princes in the Tower'.

3 Lord Audley joined the Cornish tax rebels in 1497.

4 The marriage of Prince Arthur and Catherine of Aragon was arranged by the Treaty of Medina del Campo.

Chapter 12

1 Benevolences were gifts of money made by the nobles to the King in order to secure their estates and positions.

2 The meeting between Henry VIII and Francis I in June 1520 was called the 'Field of the Cloth of Gold'.

3 Henry VIII was awarded the title *Fidei Defensor* for writing a book arguing against Martin Luther's teachings.

4 Henry VIII wanted his marriage to Catherine of Aragon to be annulled because he wanted a male heir, which Catherine seemed unable to provide.

5 The First Fruits and Tenths Act allowed Henry VIII to take a portion of the earnings of church offices.

6 The Act of Ten Articles allowed the three sacraments of baptism, penance and the Eucharist to be recognised.

Chapter 13

1 John Calvin argued for a more radical form of Protestantism than Martin Luther.

2 Lady Jane Grey unofficially reigned as Queen for nine days.

3 Wyatt's Rebellion failed mostly because Mary was able to persuade the Londoners to remain loyal to her.

4 John Foxe's *Acts and Monuments* (also known as the *Book of Martyrs*) recorded the execution of Protestants under Mary I.

Chapter 14

1 The Act of Supremacy (1559) made a small concession to Catholics by referring to Elizabeth I as the Supreme Governor of the English Church, implying that the Pope still held some authority as head of the Church.

2 Sir Francis Walsingham was the head of Elizabeth I's secret service.

3 The Battle of Gravelines was the bloodiest of the Spanish Armada campaign in 1588.

4 Hugh O'Neill led the Irish uprising against Elizabeth I between 1598 and 1602.

Chapter 15

1 Companies could obtain a monopoly by opening up new trade routes.

2 The deserving poor were those unable to work. The idle poor were those who did not work through laziness.

3 Enclosure encouraged the growth of the wool trade. Merchants then exported the wool to foreign countries, allowing the government to raise money through an export tax.

4 The wives of rich husbands had to supervise their servants and make sure that the household was being run properly.

Chapter 16

1 James I refused to dismiss the English bishops at the Hampton Court Palace conference in 1604.

2 The Addled Parliament of 1614 was dissolved because it would not agree to James I's request to raise taxes.

3 The ship money tax led to the trial of John Hampden.

4 Charles I attempted to arrest John Pym, John Hampden, Arthur Haselrig, Denzil Holles and William Strode.

Chapter 17

1 The Battle of Edgehill was fought on 23 October 1642.

2 The Marquess of Newcastle commanded the 'Whitecoats' at the Battle of Marston Moor.

3 Charles I made secret negotiations with the Scots while imprisoned in Carisbrooke Castle.

4 The decimation tax financed the local armies of the Major-Generals.

5 Charles II is supposed to have hidden in an oak tree after the Battle of Worcester in 1651.

6 The Declaration of Breda set out the terms of Charles II's restoration to the throne.

Chapter 18

1 The Convention Parliament overturned all the laws of the Interregnum.

2 The Great Fire of London started in the bakery of Thomas Farynor on Pudding Lane.

3 Charles II converted to Catholicism on his deathbed.

4 The Monmouth Rebellion was put down at the Battle of Sedgemoor in 1685.

5 William of Orange landed at Brixham, Devon, in November 1688.

Chapter 19

1 The Toleration Act (1689) allowed people to worship in private as they wished.

2 The Battle of the Boyne was fought on 12 July 1690.

3 The German allies at the Battle of Blenheim were led by Prince Eugene of Savoy.

4 The Peace of Utrecht ended the fighting between Britain and France in 1713.

5 The Act of Union came into effect in May 1707.

Chapter 20

1 Fort William, Fort Augustus and Fort George were built after the 1715 Jacobite Rebellion.

2 Sales of shares in the South Sea Company caused a stock market crash in 1720.

3 The Treaty of Seville allowed Spanish sailors to board British vessels in Spanish waters.

4 George II led the English and Hanoverian army at the Battle of Dettingen.

5 Lord George Murray advised Bonnie Prince Charlie not to fight at Culloden.

Chapter 21

1 The British made two attempts to capture Fort Duquesne in 1754 and 1755.

2 Pitt the Elder encouraged King Frederick the Great of Prussia to fight the French in Europe.

3 General Montcalm was the French commander during the Battle of the Plains of Abraham.

4 The Peace of Paris ended the Seven Years' War in 1763.

Chapter 22

1 The British government passed the Coercive Acts in response to the Boston Tea Party.

2 Major Pitcairn commanded the British during the battles of Lexington and Concord.

3 Daniel Morgan and Benedict Arnold assisted General Gates at Bemis Heights.

4 General Cornwallis defeated General Greene at the Battle of Guilford Courthouse in 1781.

Chapter 23

1 The French Parliament called itself the National Assembly after 1789.

2 *Habeas corpus* is the rule of law which holds that people cannot be arrested and held indefinitely without a trial.

3 Nelson destroyed most of the French ships at Aboukir Bay in 1798.

4 Nelson was hit and killed by a musket ball fired from the *Redoubtable*.

5 Arthur Wellesley forced the French out of Spain at the Battle of Vitoria in 1812.

6 Napoleon Bonaparte was exiled to the island of Elba in 1812.

Chapter 24

1 The 1820 conspiracy against the British government was discovered in Cato Street, London.

2 Constituencies with a very small number of voters were called 'rotten boroughs'.

3 The Duke of Wellington attempted to form a government on the resignation of Earl Grey in 1832.

4 William Lovett published the Six Points and supported the moral force.

Chapter 25

1 Robert Bakewell experimented with selective breeding in the 1760s.

2 The process by which wrought iron is produced from pig iron is called 'puddling'.

3 John Kay invented the 'flying shuttle' in 1733.

4 Matthew Boulton went into business with the inventor James Watt.

5 The contaminated water pump that caused the London cholera outbreak of 1854 was situated in Broad Street, Soho.

Chapter 26

1 The 'Rebecca Riots' took place in South Wales between 1839 and 1844.

2 Canal building in Britain stopped during the late eighteenth century because of the war in France.

3 The Liverpool and Manchester railway opened in September 1830.

4 The Clifton Suspension Bridge in Bristol was designed by Brunel.

Chapter 27

1 Granville Sharp was instrumental in first pressing for the abolition of slavery.

2 The Dolben Act prevented too many slaves from being carried on a ship.

3 Ladies' Committees were groups founded by Elizabeth Fry that visited women's prisons.

4 The Factory Act 1850 set the daily working hours for women and children as between 6am and 6pm.

Chapter 28

1 Lord George Gordon led a violent protest against Catholics in 1780.

2 Tractarians believed that Roman Catholicism, Anglicanism and Orthodoxy were the three 'branches' of a universal church.

3 John Henry Newman established oratories in Birmingham and London.

4 The Methodist districts that divided England and Wales were termed 'circuits'.

Chapter 29

1 The Bedchamber Crisis was caused by Victoria's refusal to change her household staff.

2 The Elementary Education Act 1870 established free schooling for children.

3 The building housing the Great Exhibition was called the Crystal Palace.

4 Mary Seacole set up the British Hotel near Sevastopol.

5 Florence Nightingale was given the nickname the 'Lady with the Lamp'.

6 Emily Wilding Davison was killed attempting a protest at the Epsom Derby in 1913.

Chapter 30

1 Robert Clive won the Battle of Plassey in 1757.

2 Bahadur Shah II was the Mughal Emperor at the time of the Indian Mutiny.

3 The Boers referred to outsiders living in the Transvaal as 'Uitlanders'.

4 General Cronje surrendered his Boer soldiers at the siege of Paardeberg in 1900.

5 Britain and France signed the Entente Cordiale in 1904.

Appendix 1 – Timelines

The monarchs of England, 1066–1485

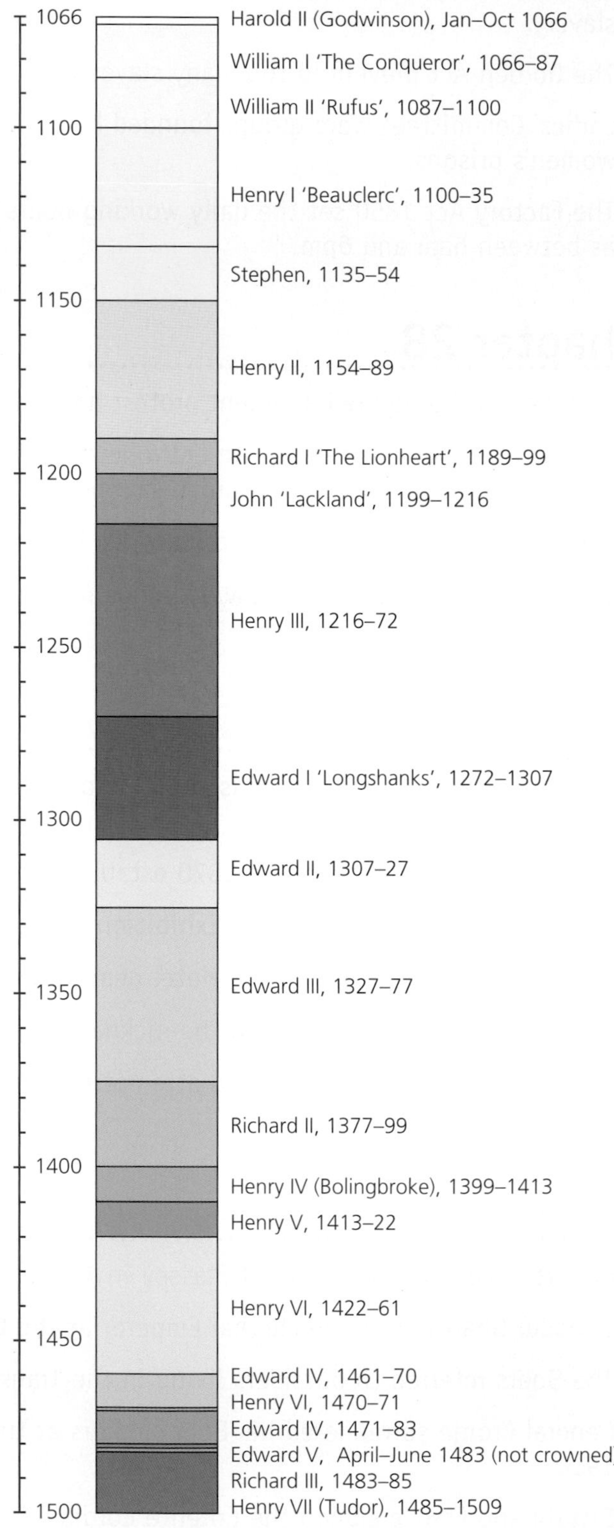

The monarchs of England, 1485–1750

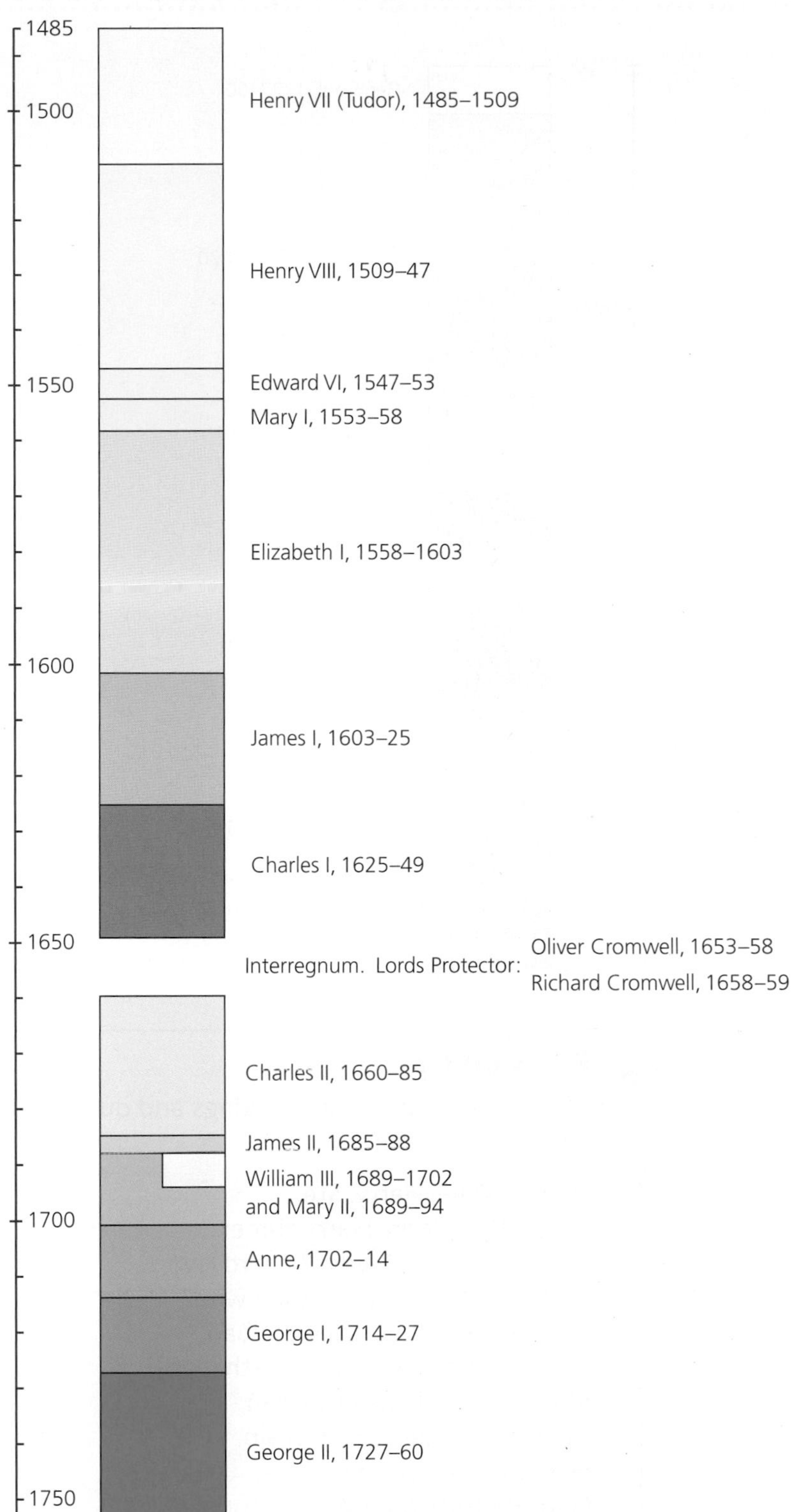

The monarchs of Great Britain and the United Kingdom, 1750–1900

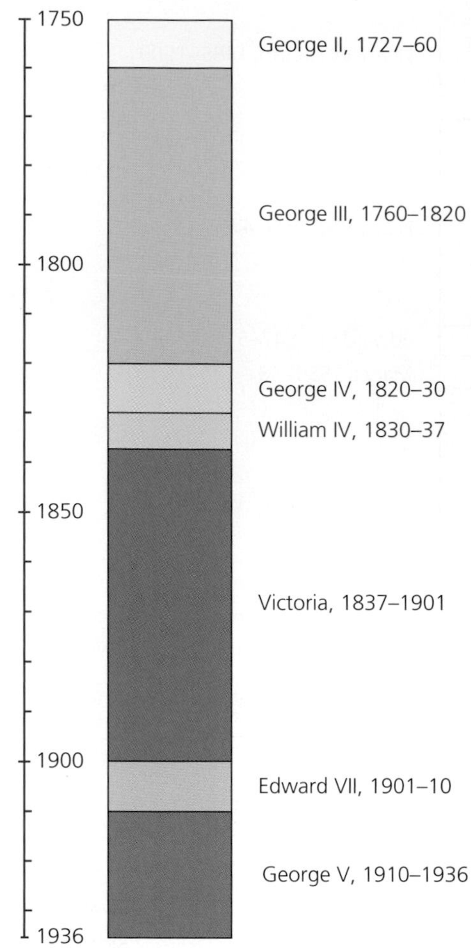

Revision tip

To help you remember the kings and queens of England, there is an old childhood rhyme:

Willie, Willie, Harry, Ste,
Harry, Dick, John, Harry three;
One, two, three Neds, Richard two,
Harrys four, five, six ... then who?
Edwards four, five, Dick the bad,
Harrys (twain*), then Ned (the lad);
Mary, Bessie, James the vain,
Charlie, Charlie, James again.
Will and Mary, Anna Gloria,
Georges four, then Will, Victoria;
Edward seven, George and Ted,
George the sixth, now Liz instead.

* Note that twain means two.

Learn this by heart and you will never forget who ruled when ever again.

Appendix 2 – Family trees

Dates of reigns are given in bold.

For Chapters 1–2

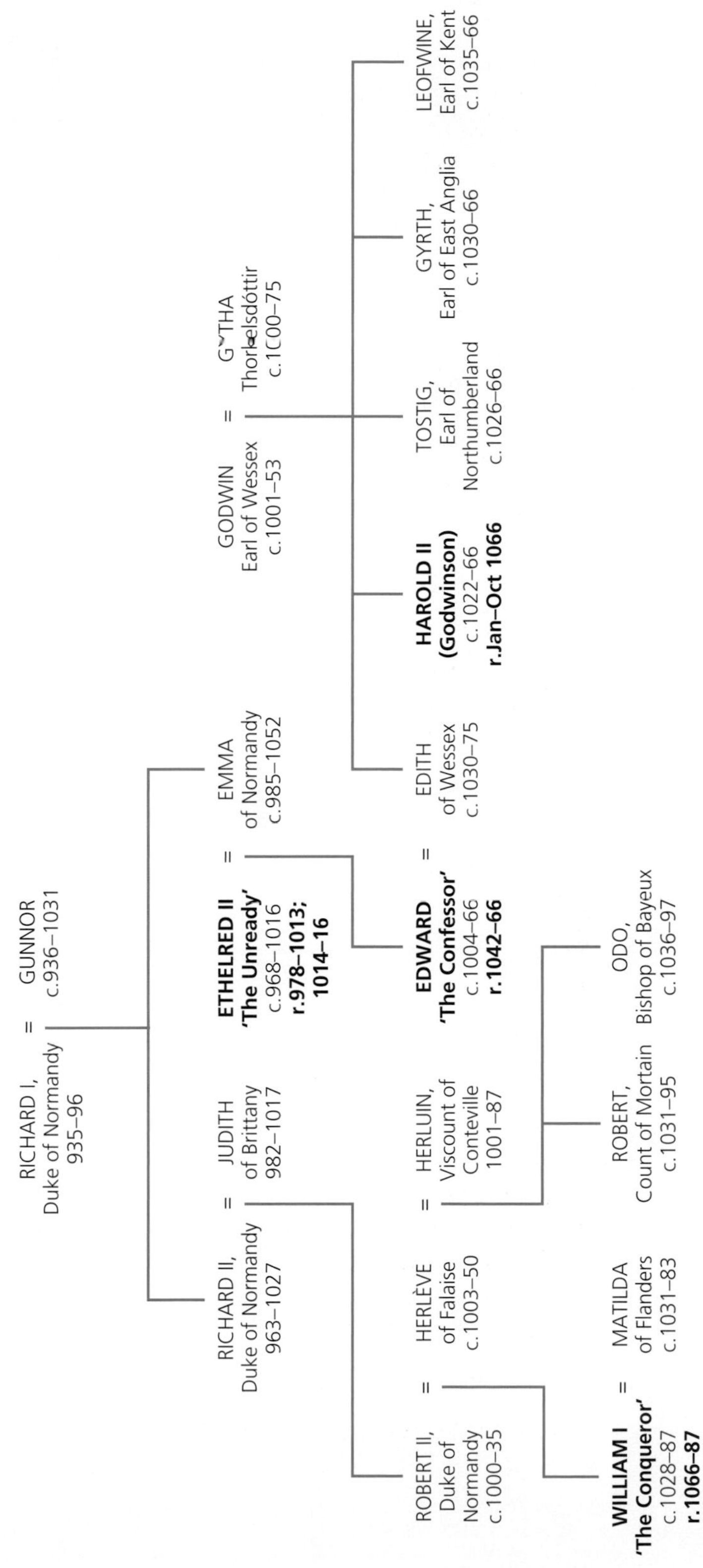

For Chapters 3–5

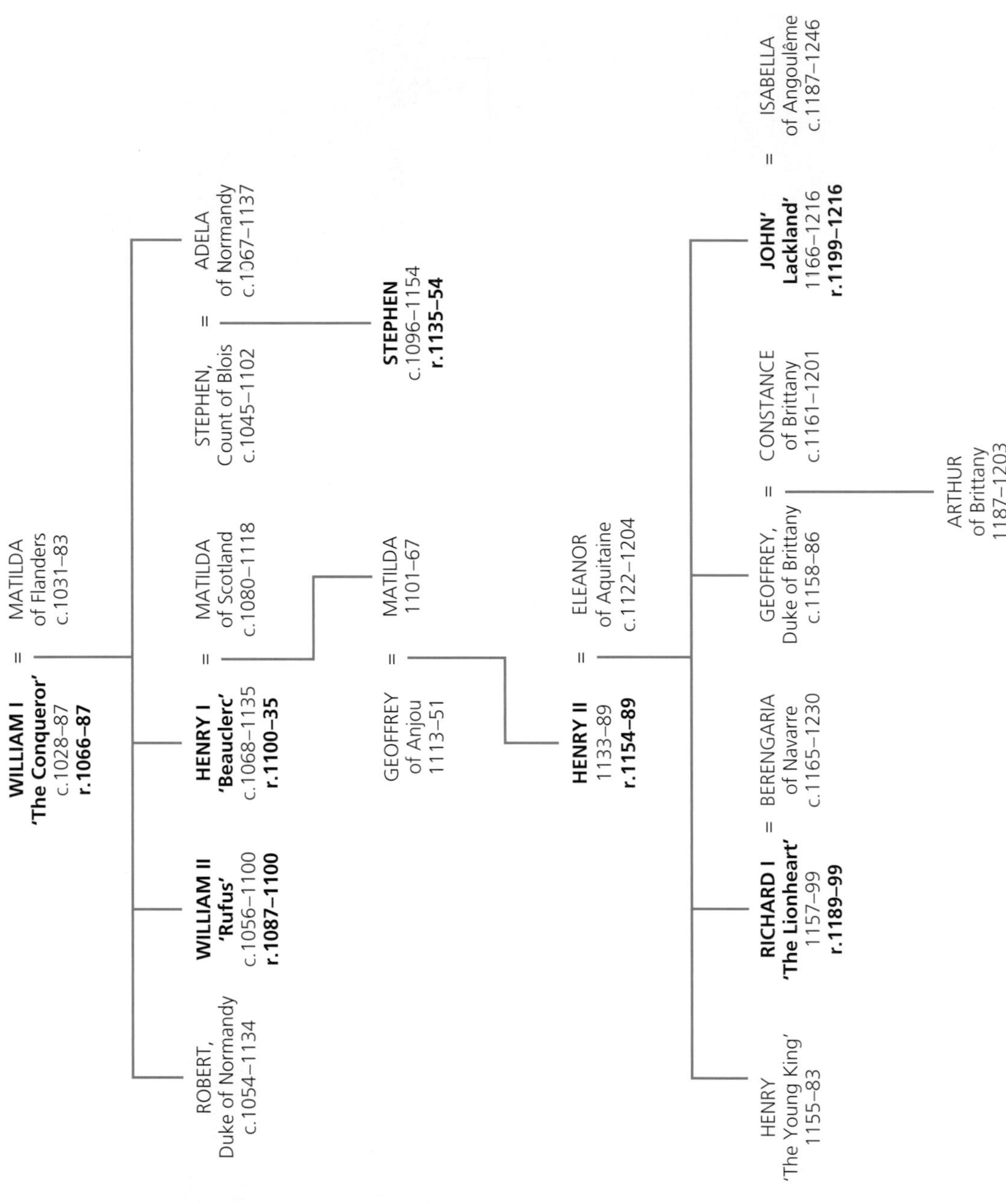

For Chapter 6

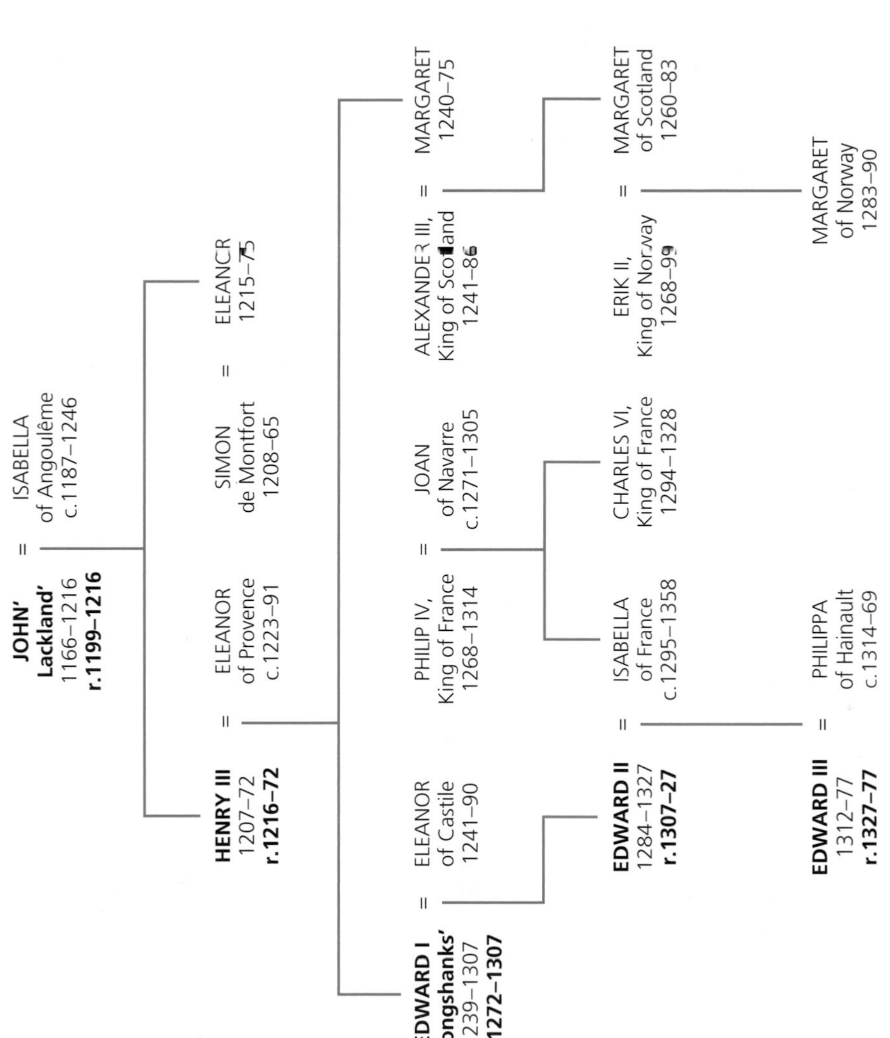

For Chapters 8–11

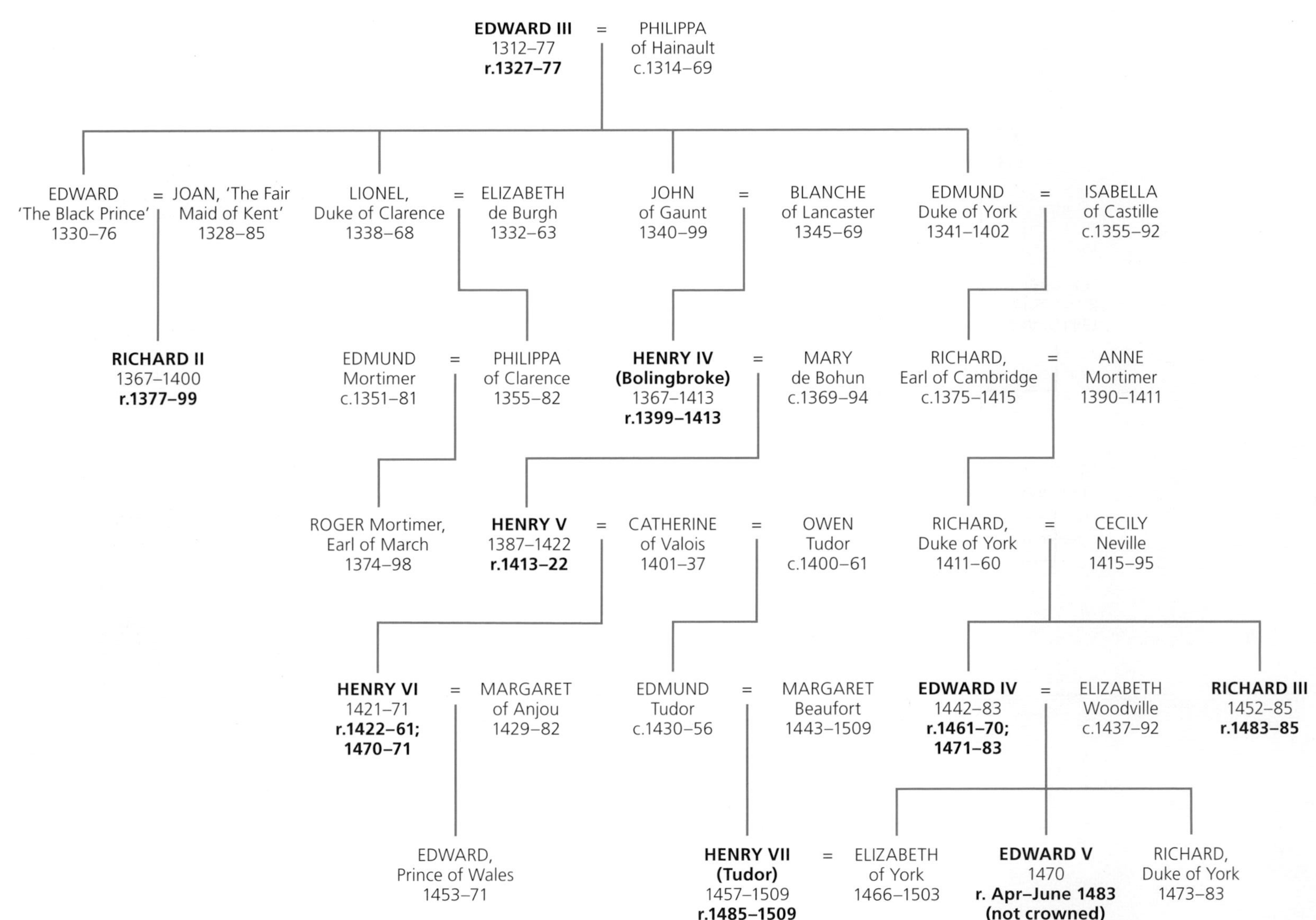

For Chapters 12–14

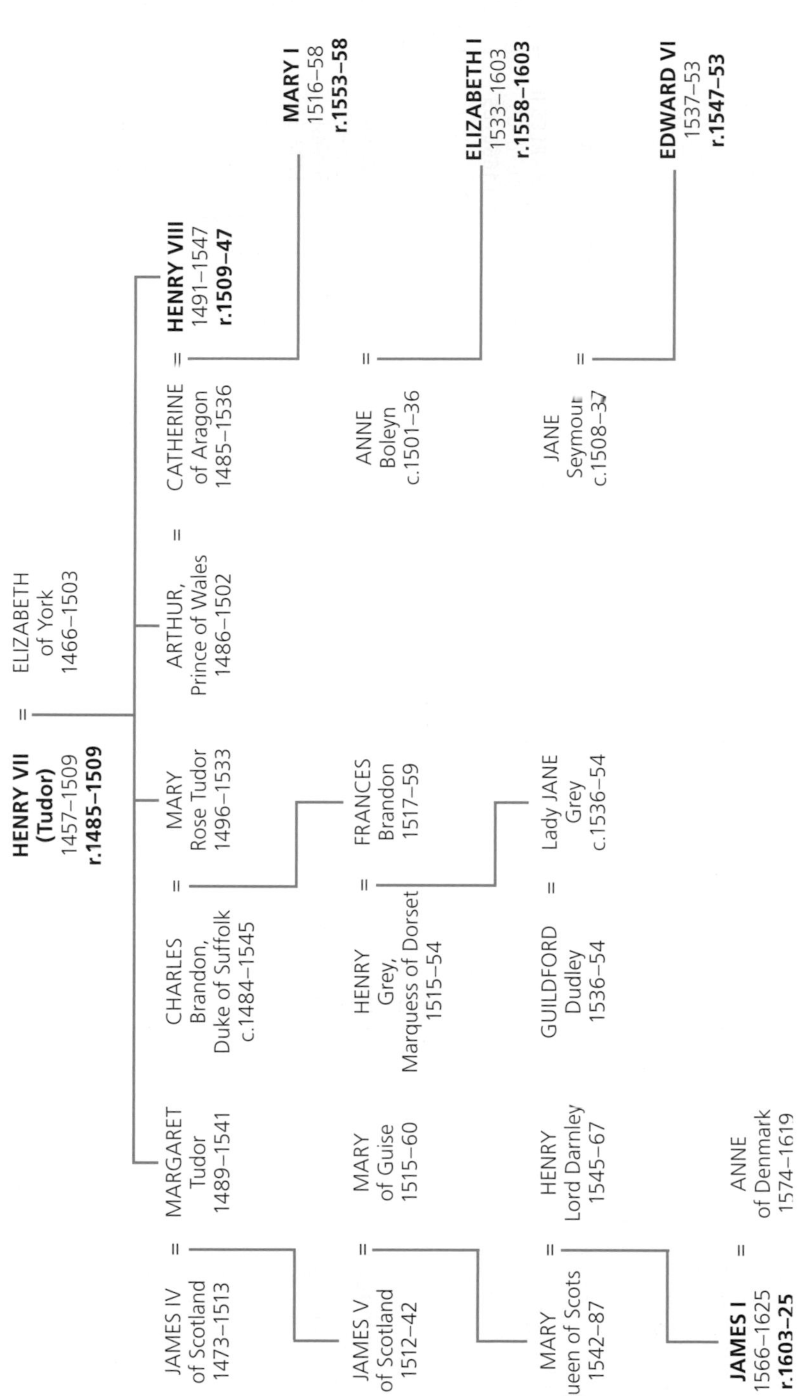

For Chapters 16–20

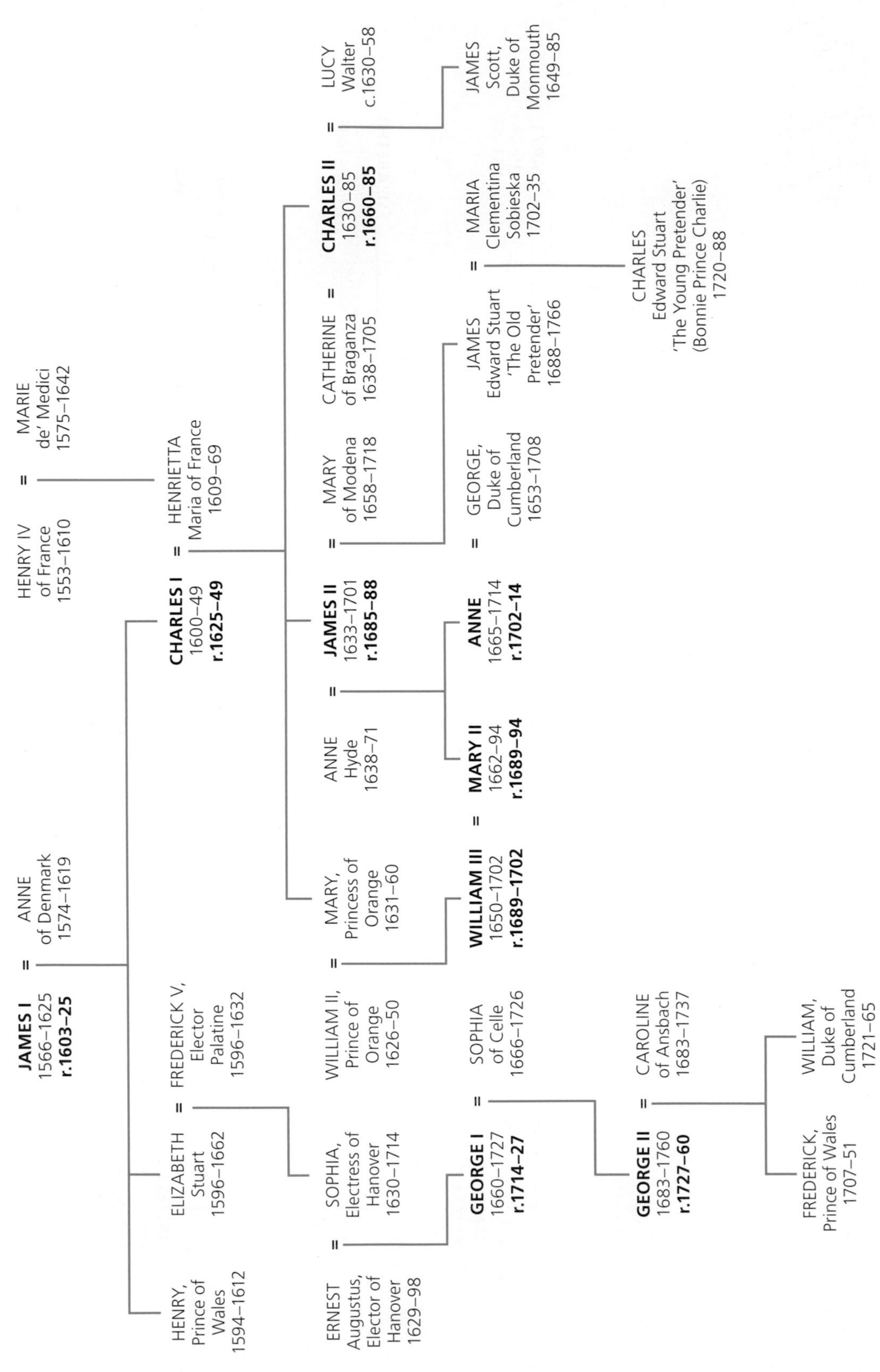